Discover the Gifts of the Holy Spirit
the LIGHT Seminar Plus

To Carmen:
May God renew the Power of The Holy Spirit within you!

— Dcn. Michael ...

Pg 104 — Intercessory Prayer

Discovering
the Gifts
of the
Holy Spirit
the LIGHT Seminar Plus

Deacon Michael Wesley

outskirts press

Discovering the Gifts of the Holy Spirit
the LIGHT Seminar Plus
All Rights Reserved.
Copyright © 2022 Deacon Michael Wesley
v5.0 r1.0

The opinions expressed in this manuscript are solely the opinions of the author and do not represent the opinions or thoughts of the publisher. The author has represented and warranted full ownership and/or legal right to publish all the materials in this book.

This book may not be reproduced, transmitted, or stored in whole or in part by any means, including graphic, electronic, or mechanical without the express written consent of the publisher except in the case of brief quotations embodied in critical articles and reviews.

Outskirts Press, Inc.
http://www.outskirtspress.com

ISBN: 978-1-9772-5570-9

Cover Photo © 2022 www.gettyimages.com. All rights reserved - used with permission.

Outskirts Press and the "OP" logo are trademarks belonging to Outskirts Press, Inc.

PRINTED IN THE UNITED STATES OF AMERICA

Copyright Permissions

Sounds of Wonder: Speaking in Tongues in the Catholic Tradition by Eddie Ensley. Copyright ©1977 by Eddie Ensley. Published by Paulist Press, Inc., New York/Mahwah, NJ. www.paulistpress.com. Used with permission of Paulist Press.

Christian Initiation and Baptism in the Holy Spirit: Evidence from the First Eight Centuries. By Killian McDonnell and George T. Montague. Collegeville, MN. The Liturgical Press, 1994. Used with permission.

Vatican Council II: The Conciliar and Postconciliar Documents by Austin Flannery, O.P (ed.) New Revised Edition. Collegeville, MN., Liturgical Press. 1996. Used with permission.

Permission for Papal quotes given by Libreria Editrice Vaticana, May 15, 2020.

The writings of Mother Teresa of Calcutta © by the Mother Teresa Center, exclusive licensee throughout the world of the Missionaries of Charity for the works of Mother Teresa. Used with permission.

Excerpts from the English translation of the Catechism of the Catholic Church for use in the United States of America Copyright © 1994, United States Catholic Conference, Inc.—Libreria Editrice Vaticana. Used with Permission. English translation of the Catechism of the Catholic Church: Modifications from the Editio Typica copyright © 1997, United States Conference of Catholic Bishops—Libreria Editrice Vaticana.

Permission has been obtained from the Institute of Carmelite Studies for the quotes from St. John of the Cross and St. Teresa of Avila.

Unless otherwise noted, all scriptures are from the NEW AMERICAN BIBLE© 2010, 1991, 1986, 1970 Confraternity of Christian Doctrine, Washington, D.C. and are used by permission of the copyright owner.

All Rights Reserved. No part of the New American Bible may be reproduced in any form without permission in writing from the copyright owner.

Scripture quotations marked (RSV) are taken from the REVISED STANDARD VERSION, Grand Rapids: Zondervan, 1971. Used by permission. All rights reserved.

Excerpts from The Jerusalem Bible (JB), copyrighted © 1966 by Darton, Longman & Todd Ltd., and Doubleday, a division of Bantam Doubleday Dell Publishing Group, Inc. Reprinted by permission.

Abbreviations.

CCC: Catechism of the Catholic Church

JB: The 1966 translation of the Jerusalem Bible

Jn: The Gospel of John.

KJV: King James Version

NAB: The New American Bible translation.

RSV: The Revised Standard Version

Dedication Page

This book is dedicated to the greater glory of God and to my wife, Kathy, who is one of God's greatest gifts to me.

"Glory be to him whose power, working in us, can do infinitely more than we can ask or imagine."

-Ephesians 3:20–21, Jerusalem Bible

Acknowledgements

I would like to thank the following people for their help in the production of this book: Fr. Bob Hogan, BBD, Sr. Miriam Grady, DLJC, Mary Quinalty, Joseph Cieszinski, MTS, Andrew Ortiz, Art Garcia, Ethel Garcia, Nestor and Nellie Baca, Vincent Montoya, Deacon Frank Smith, Kathy Wesley, Marcella Gibson, Betty Braswell, Jane Zingelman, Patricia Gutierrez, Tim Fresquez, and John Fidel (of happy memory).

Table of Contents

Acknowledgements i
Foreword v
Introduction vii
1. What the World Needs Now 1
2. My Discovery of the Gifts of the Holy Spirit 6
3. The Gifts in Church History 14
4. The Church's Re-discovery of the Holy Spirit 21
5. Discovering the Isaiah 11:2-3 Gifts 32
6. Discovering the Cardinal Virtues 54
7. Discovering the Word Gifts 65
8. Discovering the Gifts of Power 76
9. Discovering the Gifts of Revelation 88
10. Discovering the Gifts of Service: Mercy, Hospitality,
    Giving, Leadership, and Serving in Ministry 99
11. Discovering the Ephesians 4:11 Gifts:
    Apostleship, Evangelization, and Pastoring 110
12. Overcoming Obstacles to Living the
    Spirit-filled Life 120
13. The Prayer of Forgiveness 132
14. Discovering Daily Growth 145
15. Spiritual Warfare 161
16. Scriptural Helps 178
17. The Invitation 182
Bibliography 184

Foreword

In *Discovering the Gifts of the Holy Spirit* Deacon Michael R. Wesley seeks to help Catholics grow in their understanding of the Holy Spirit and the gifts of the Spirit. He has known many Catholics who have had an experience of spiritual renewal in their lives through movements like the ACTS retreat, Cursillo, RCIA, youth retreats, etc. Their experience is similar to those who have gone through a Life in the Spirit Seminar through Charismatic Renewal groups. Their faith is more alive, and they have a greater desire to share their faith with others.

Often what is missing is an understanding of how to allow the Holy Spirit to work in one's life for service and evangelization through the gifts of the Spirit ("charisms" is the word in Greek used in the New Testament that is translated as "gifts of the Spirit").

Deacon Michael explains both the gifts of the Spirit found in Isaiah 11 and the charismatic gifts found in the New Testament. The seven gifts of the Spirit found in Isaiah 11 are more commonly known and taught in the Catholic Church. Building on the teaching of the Second Vatican Council, all the popes since the Council have emphasized the importance of refocusing on the importance of the charismatic gifts, which commonly have not been explained well in the Catholic teaching.

This book will help you to understand and experience both the Isaiah 11 gifts and the charismatic gifts. Deacon Michael gives practical guidance and examples in how to become more open to the working of the Holy Spirit, and how to overcome obstacles to living fully in the Spirit. He explains the individual gifts and helps us see their value for our lives. I have often said in my teaching that if God has given you a responsibility or "calling," you should seek the spiritual empowerment (spiritual gifts) that will allow God to work through you to complete your God-given responsibility or "calling." This book is a wonderful aid that can enable us to allow the Holy Spirit to accomplish God's work in our lives.

—Fr. Bob Hogan. BBD

Fr. Bob has taught Theology at two Catholic Universities. He is the author of a book on the charismatic dimension of the Church and charismatic renewal, Celebrating a Charismatic Jubilee. *He is the former chairperson of the National Service Committee for Catholic Charismatic Renewal in the USA. He is presently a member of CHARIS National Service of Communion USA, which is the USA branch of the new structure that Pope Francis has organized for Catholic Charismatic Renewal throughout the world.*

Introduction

In my previous book, the LIGHT Seminar: Living in the Gifts of the Holy Trinity, I described some of the gifts of the Holy Spirit and how they can be used in everyday life. The current book, *Discovering the Gifts of the Holy Spirit,* covers the same material but with more information and stories of people using the gifts of the Holy Spirit. So, if you have read *the LIGHT Seminar,* you can still benefit from reading this new version.

For most of you, though, this will be a brand-new read. One question that might come to you is, is this book really necessary? Most Catholics learn about the Holy Spirit's gifts in Confirmation or RCIA. Is there any point in going over it again? I want to preface my answer with a personal story.

Very early one morning, when I was nine years old, I saw my dad asleep on the couch with the television turned on. I don't know why I got up, but I found myself in a unique situation. Having never watched television in the wee hours of the morning before, I saw this as an adventure! So, I sat on the floor and began watching the program my dad had been viewing.

The movie he had been watching was *Joan of Arc,* starring Ingrid Bergman. I must have been impressed by Ms.

Bergman's portrayal because I decided I wanted to be a saint. My only problem was I had no idea how to do this. But there was one thing I remembered from the story. The attire Joan of Arc wore looked a lot like my pajamas. With this awareness came the idea of how I could become a saint; I'd dress like one!

So, I decided that if I wore my pajamas to school every day, I would become a saint. It seems like a silly idea now, but at the time it made a lot of sense. I knew my mom wouldn't let me wear my pajamas to school, though, even if it was to make me a saint. So, I devised a scheme where I'd put my pajamas on under my school uniform, change clothes before getting to school and change into my regular clothes before returning home.

What I failed to consider was where was I going to change my clothes on the way to school and keep them all day long? And it never even occurred to me that the nuns wouldn't let me spend the day at school in my pajamas. *My plan had left out some very important parts.*

So, the next day I tried sneaking out of the house with my saintly-looking pajamas under my school uniform. But as I said goodbye to my mom, she caught sight of the bulge underneath my corduroy pants. She checked inside my pants and, seeing the pajamas, ordered me to take them off and never do that again! She probably thought I was border lining childhood insanity.

I'm sharing this story because if you ask many people about the gifts of the Holy Spirit, they will probably leave out some very important parts as well. Quite often, high school students enroll in Confirmation classes. They may be sincere in their efforts but are more concerned about school, sports, relationships, hobbies, and extra-curricular activities. They attend the class because their parents want them to or so they can get married in the Church. They go through the motions, but their hearts are not into it. There are exceptions, but this is the general rule.

RCIA participants are often sincere and enthusiastic about learning the faith. However, they are more concerned with raising children, making a living, family responsibilities, and sometimes continuing their education. So much is going on in their lives that they might not remember everything covered about the gifts of the Holy Spirit.

Even if they do remember everything about the gifts, there often isn't time to do more than a cursory examination during a class. Then there is the group of Catholics who never were Confirmed. They would never have learned about the gifts of the Holy Spirit in an elementary religion class. Even products of a Catholic education probably fall short in their understanding of the gifts of the Holy Spirit.

These are some reasons why a book like this is needed. What happens with many people is similar to my experience. I stopped attending Mass in high school because it didn't seem to have anything to do with life. As I later discovered, our relationship with God has everything to do with life!

God wants us to have an abundant life (John 10:10), he has a wonderful plan prepared for us (Jeremiah 29:11-12,) and he is constantly drawing us towards that abundance (John 10:10.) When the Holy Spirit comes to *life* within us, we become more aware of God's gifts, and his call to serve. We become participants with Jesus in continuing his ministry on earth.

The purpose of the Holy Spirit is to make Jesus's presence real to us and to make his presence real to the world. This will be covered in the next chapter, *What the World Needs Now.*

CHAPTER 1
What the World Needs Now

In 1965 Hal David and Burt Bacharach composed a song that was later made a hit by Jackie DeShannon called, *What the World Needs Now.* The song is a prayer to God, asking him to send love to the world because that's the one thing we need more than anything else. Never was a truer statement made.

The irony is that God has sent love into the world through his Son, Jesus Christ. In 1 John 4:16, we're told that God is love and Colossians 1:15 further adds that "(Jesus) is the image of the invisible God" (NAB.) Love has come to the world in the person of Jesus Christ!

Just before Jesus's ascension into heaven, he said, "And behold, I am with you always, until the end of the age." What Jesus meant by this statement is that he will be with us forever. As we're reminded in Hebrews 13:8: "Jesus Christ is the same today as he was yesterday and as he will be forever" (JB 1966.) But the question is, if Jesus is here, then where is he?

Our faith teaches that we were created for God (CCC 27,) and the only way to God is through Jesus Christ (Jn. 14:6.) One of the reasons there may be so much turmoil in the world is because people are hungering to know God through his Son, and they don't know where to find him.

That's where we come in. As Jesus was the visible image of the unseen God, we are the visible image of Jesus Christ. People should see Jesus through our love for each other (Jn. 13:35) and our use of the gifts of the Holy Spirit.

In John 14:12, Jesus told his disciples, "Amen, amen, I say to you, whoever believes in me will do the works that I do, and will do greater ones than these, because I am going to the Father" (NAB.) Jesus was telling his apostles [as he tells us] to continue ministering in the same way he did; through teaching, healing, performing miracles (1 Corinthians 12,) casting out evil spirits (Luke 10:17,) and evangelization (Matthew 28:19.)

In John 10b–11, Jesus said, "The Father who dwells in me is doing his works. Believe me that I am in the Father and the Father is in me, or else, believe because of the works themselves" (NAB.) The gifts of the Holy Spirit are the works of Jesus flowing through us. We should be able to tell people, "If you don't believe me because of my words, believe because of the works that you see flowing through me."

St. Paul gives a maxim in Galatians 2:20 for being Jesus's disciples. He said, "It is no longer I who live, but Christ who lives in me" (RSV.) When people see us, they should see Jesus Christ. Jesus attracted people because of what he said and did. People should still be attracted to Jesus by the things we say and do.

If it was important for Jesus to accompany his words with works, it is essential for us to do the same. We may not be as sensitive to the Holy Spirit as Jesus was, but the Holy Spirit can still work through us in bringing Jesus's presence to others. One of the ways he does this is through his gifts.

Gifts and Talents

It is important to remember that there is a difference between a gift of the Holy Spirit and a natural gift or talent. Someone may, for instance, be an outstanding basketball player. They have a certain genetic ability for athletics, and they probably spent several hours fine-tuning their skill. They can thank God for their natural ability because "every perfect gift is from above" (James 1:17, NAB). However, basketball players will still have their athletic ability whether or not they have the Holy Spirit.

The reason we receive the gifts of the Holy Spirit is so we can continue ministering in Jesus's name. A natural ability for playing sports, academics, entertainment, or any skill alone will not win souls for Jesus Christ. The purpose of the gifts of the Holy Spirit is so we can win others for Jesus.

Now, it is true that a gift of the Holy Spirit can be added to someone's natural ability. For instance, someone with a natural gift of teaching can also receive an anointed gift for instructing children in the faith. Once someone has surrendered an innate ability to Jesus, the Lord will often anoint that skill, using it for his purpose. That's why St. Paul encourages us to "do everything in the name of the Lord Jesus" (Colossians 3:17.) But it can also happen that someone without a natural gift for teaching can become an anointed teacher through the gift of the Holy Spirit.

For instance, a parishioner may learn there is a need for teachers in the catechetical program at her parish. She had never thought about teaching before or ever taught a class. Suddenly, there is a quickening in her heart. She contacts the religious education director, and before she knows it, she's teaching a class. It might be difficult for her, but eventually, she begins to catch on. She perseveres, and suddenly, a gift for teaching begins to emerge.

Spiritual gifts, just like natural gifts, grow with their use. We often begin to use natural gifts because we have a certain facility for them. Spiritual gifts emerge because we are drawn to serving in a certain way. We may not have a natural skill for that task, but a hunger in the heart motivates us to act. This can happen with leadership, administration, serving, or with any of the gifts of the Holy Spirit.

Sometimes these gifts are obvious, and sometimes they are harder to see. A parishioner told me he has a gift for leadership because he often finds himself in leadership positions. He never considered this skill a gift of the Holy Spirit, but it suddenly became obvious to him that it was.

Sometimes our gifts will be pointed out to us by someone else. Several years ago, a friend told me I have the gift of having mercy. As I'll share later, that was not what I wanted to hear at the time, but mercy is a gift of the Holy Spirit.

My pastor claims that I have a gift for preaching. I've seen myself preach on TV, and I'm not convinced, but I'll take his word for it. He's encouraging this gift that he sees in me. We can also ask God for a gift we would like to have. There is no guarantee he will give us that gift, but we can rest assured God will give us the gift or gifts he wants us to have.

In Matthew 25:31-46, Jesus tells the parable of the sheep and the goats. He summarizes the story's two sections with, "whatever you did for one of these least brothers of mine, you did for me (Matthew 25: 40 and 45.) I believe there are two meanings to this expression. In the same way that we are doing these things *to* Jesus, we are also doing them *for* him. Since Jesus is not here to do them on his own, we are his ambassadors (2 Corinthians 5:20.)

Jesus wants us to be his hands and feet, so he can continue ministering to others through us. One avenue God has given us for this is through the gifts of the Holy Spirit. Although God can use our natural abilities, the gifts of the Holy Spirit are separate from them.

CHAPTER 2

My Discovery of the Gifts of the Holy Spirit

I think I was in third grade when I first heard about the day of Pentecost.[1] At the time, I was attending a Catholic School in southern California.

Our teacher told us that the Holy Spirit had come down upon the early believers and empowered them with such courage and love that many gladly gave their lives for God. They were filled with tremendous joy, and their love for each other radiated from their hearts. There were miracles, healings, and the grace of the Holy Spirit abounded among them!

I remember getting excited about it and thinking, "Wow, this is really neat! Maybe this is something I can experience too!" But then the teacher completely popped my bubble when she said, "Of course, this doesn't happen anymore." That may not be what she meant or perhaps even what she said, but that's how I remember it. In any case, it left me

---

1   Pentecost is a Jewish feast commemorating Moses receiving the Ten Commandments on Mt. Sinai. During this feast, Jesus's first followers received the outpouring of the Holy Spirit. It's called *the birthday of the Church.*

believing that the Pentecostal experience was for an era long past.

Ten years later, I attended Eastern New Mexico University in Roswell. I had left my Catholic roots by this time because I didn't see the Church answering any of the questions I had about life.

During my second semester at Eastern, I met a young man (I'll call him Steve) who was the same age I was. At first, we seemed to have a lot in common: An interest in philosophy, contemporary music, and social issues. So, when he asked to meet with me that evening to continue our discussion, it seemed like a good idea.

I thought we would talk about philosophy, drugs, music, girls, and the crucial things in life. When we met that evening, there was an older guy with Steve. He must have been in his thirties. (I'll call him Frank.) I wondered what the heck he was doing there! I eventually discovered that Frank was a Baptist charismatic Christian and Steve was a Catholic charismatic Christian.

Their initial intention was simply to share Jesus with me. Friends may have told them I was living a wild, senseless lifestyle and needed Jesus. I'm not sure why they chose to take me under their wings, but there I was arguing with Steve about the pros and cons of Christianity. He seemed to have a better grasp of information than I did, but I was holding my own. But then Frank brought out the big guns!

He looked over at me and said, "Mike, there's a tape I want to play for you." He played a reel-to-reel recording of people sharing about an experience they had called baptism in the Holy Spirit. God had filled them with a tremendous awareness of his love for them. Peace and joy radiated from their hearts, and they each had received various gifts of the Holy Spirit!

As I listened to the tape, I was suddenly back in third grade when I was told that the experience of Pentecost was a thing of the past. Now I was being told that Pentecost is still very much alive! The only way Frank could have known the significance that tape would have for me was by the Holy Spirit. All I wanted to know now was how I could receive the baptism in the Holy Spirit.

We talked more about a personal relationship with Jesus Christ and the Spirit-filled life. Now I was ready to listen. That night outside my dormitory room, I asked Jesus Christ to come into my heart and be the Lord of my life. There were no fireworks or bubbly feelings of joy but a quiet peace that let me know God had heard my prayer.

Shortly after that, I purchased my first bible. In my dormitory room that night, I randomly opened the bible, and my eyes fell on these words: "I know the plans I have in mind for you—it is Yahweh who speaks—plans for peace, not disaster, reserving a future full of hope for you" (Jeremiah 29:11–12, JB).

That was a significant passage because I had recently concluded that I had no hope in life. I had moved in with some friends off-campus; we called ourselves freaks. Consequently, I was flunking most of my classes and seemed to be making the same mistakes I always had. I wasn't happy, I had not been for a while, and it seemed like I never would be.

I decided that my lot in life was to be a loser; nothing could change that. But now God was telling me I had a future full of hope? Only the Holy Spirit could have opened the Bible to the exact passage I needed to read. Now, I don't think we should randomly open the bible expecting to see God's answer to every question we have. Still, in this situation, I believe it was the power of the Holy Spirit turning those pages of scripture. I received an incredible sense of peace and joy.

About two weeks after that, I attended a conference of the Full Gospel Businessman's Fellowship in Midland, Texas.[2] The keynote speaker was Lt. Col. Merlin Carothers. I had recently read his book, *Prison to Praise*, and I wanted to hear him speak. Another reason I had for going, though, was to be baptized in the Holy Spirit. I thought that it was only at a conference like this that one could have this experience.

So, I took all my money and purchased two bus tickets to Midland, Texas. Steve was going to accompany me. It

---

2 The *Full Gospel Businessman's Fellowship International* is an interdenominational organization of men and women whose lives have been changed through the experience of baptism in the Holy Spirit.

literally was a journey of faith as the thought of a registration fee had not even occurred to us. We had no idea where we would stay, how we would eat, or how we would get back to Roswell. We believed that God was going to provide.

The only part of the conference I remember attending was Saturday evening. Hundreds of people in a large auditorium were praising God with arms raised. They were praying in tongues,[3] spending moments in silence, occasionally speaking out in prophecy. I remember hearing a beautiful prophecy [4] about God pouring his gifts out on the earth like torrents of rain falling from the sky. The words flowed so smoothly and eloquently that I knew they had come from the prophet's heart.

Lt. Col. Merlin Carothers then spoke on the importance of praising God at all times and in all situations. Basing his teaching on two texts of Scripture, Romans 8:28 [5] and 1 Thessalonians 5:18,[6] his message was that God will work in all things for the good when we praise him for them. Then he asked those wanting to receive the baptism in the Holy Spirit to come forward.

---

[3] We will discuss the gift of tongues more in chapter 7.
[4] Prophecy is a gift that will be discussed more in chapter 9.
[5] "We know that all things work for good for those who love God… (NAB.)
[6] "In all circumstances give thanks, for this is the will of God for you in Christ Jesus (NAB.)

I was hesitant about stepping forward because of the crowds and perhaps a feeling of unworthiness. But he kept calling out, "There is still someone else." Finally, I stepped forward. A middle-aged man laid his hand on my shoulder as they began to pray for us.

What I experienced that night was a deep sense of depression. I recognize now that this was the devil's attempt to discourage me, but at the time, I was confused. Where was the joy, and where were the gifts I was supposed to receive?

That night I was very depressed. The thought that kept coming to me was that I was unworthy of being loved by God. That's why I didn't receive the blessing I had expected. But then I remembered the teaching of Merlin Carothers to praise God at all times and in all situations.

So, I began to follow his instruction. I began to praise God that I felt so depressed. I thanked him for not loving me or granting me his baptism in the Holy Spirit. I praised him that I felt so confused.

But as I continued to go through the motions of praising God, I suddenly became aware of the joy in my heart. There was a peace I had never known, and I knew God loved me. I had received the experience of baptism in the Holy Spirit.

The Midland family we stayed with that evening had a tremendous gift of hospitality. They gave us a change of clothes, let us sleep while they went to church, bought us lunch, and purchased two bus tickets back to Roswell. God did provide for us. About two weeks later, I received the gift of tongues.

This testimony is how I began opening up to the gifts of the Holy Spirit. It is important to note that baptism in the Holy Spirit is not an addition to the sacraments of initiation. It is simply the fruit of the sacraments coming to life in a believer's spirituality.

"As each one has received a gift, use it to serve one another as good stewards of God's varied grace"

-1 Peter 4:10-NAB

CHAPTER 3
The Gifts in Church History

It is interesting to see how the use of some of the gifts of the Holy Spirit have evolved throughout Church history. The story begins in the book of Acts with Jesus's followers having a life-changing encounter with the Holy Spirit.

They were hiding from the Jewish authorities, fearing torture for their association with Jesus. They were also seeking a sign from God to let them know what they should do. Jesus had been their guide for the last three years, and they had hoped he would become the king of Israel. Even before his ascension into heaven, the apostles asked, "Lord, are you at this time going to restore the kingdom to Israel?" (Acts 1:6, NAB)

When the day of Pentecost came, they were praying in an upper room. Suddenly, there was the sound of a strong wind, and tongues of fire appeared on each one of them. They were all filled with the Holy Spirit and began worshipping God in languages none of them knew. We'll discuss these languages more in the chapter on the word gifts. But it can safely be said that they were overwhelmed with joy as they boldly proclaimed God's praises.

Some believe only the apostles were present in the upper room on the day of Pentecost. Scripture does tell us, though, that at least 120 of Jesus's followers were gathered for the selection of Matthias to replace Judas Iscariot. It is logical to assume this same group was praying together on the day of Pentecost.

So, when they all made their united, joyful sound, many of the people were drawn to it. They wondered what all the raucous was about! Remember, Pentecost was one of three feasts where every Jewish man was required to offer a sacrifice in Jerusalem if it was at all possible for him to do so. Consequently, there would have been a multitude of people listening to this sound.

At this point, Peter opened up to his gift of teaching and preaching. This man, who had three times denied that he even knew Jesus stood up before the Jewish multitude. He preached a sermon so powerful that three thousand souls were added that day (Acts 2:41).

In the days following, that number grew to five thousand men (Acts 4:4), to say nothing of women and children. The growth was due to the change people saw in the believer's lives and the wonderous works done at the apostle's hands. (See Acts 2:43 as an example of the community that had formed.)

The Gifts Since the Early Days

Even though the book of Acts speaks of the unity that existed in the early Church, we know this wasn't always the case. Each community had its own share of problems. In addressing these problems, one of the topics Paul brought up in his letters was the gifts of the Holy Spirit.

Paul talked about the gifts he saw present in the Church of his day: prophecy, tongues, the interpretation of tongues, healing, and miracles. We rarely see these gifts in our own time. Were they meant only to establish the early Church as some theologians teach? If this is true then when, why, and how did these gifts stop functioning in the church-or did they?

In the Didache, which is a church document dating from the first to the early second century CE, there is a description of how a community can recognize a true prophet.[7] During the first century, Justin Martyr (100–165 CE) believed the charismatic gifts were still active in the Church and would be until the end of time.[8] St. Irenaeus (120–200 CE) believed that not only did charismatic gifts exist during his time but that one could never count all the gifts of the Holy Spirit.[9]

Tertullian (155–240 CE) believed newly baptized adults received charismatic gifts by asking for them.[25] Eusebius (260–339 CE) wrote in his commentary on the Psalms that

---

7   The Didache, 11.7–11.12.
8   Yves Congar, *I Believe in the Holy Spirit*, Book 1 (New York: Herder Crossroad, 2005), 65.
9   McDonnell and Montague, *Christian Initiation and Baptism in the Holy Spirit*, Second Revised Edition, Collegeville, MN. The Liturgical Press. 1994. 357.

the church still possessed the charismatic gifts, including "the word of wisdom, the word of knowledge, faith, healings, and tongues."[10]

St. Hillary of Poitiers (315–367 CE) believed the charismatic gifts of the Holy Spirit were still active in his day, as he mentions them several times in his work, *On the Trinity*.[11] He also taught that when a person is baptized, the Lord has pity on them in their weakness and feeds them spiritually with the seven gifts of the Holy Spirit: wisdom, understanding, counsel, strength, knowledge, piety, and fear of the Lord.[28] St. Hillary saw the Isaiah and charismatic gifts as a part of the Christian experience.

By the end of the fourth century, though, the charismatic gifts seem to have decreased in the Church. There were still gifts of teaching, leadership, ministry, and dispositions of holiness. Miracles were still taking place,[12] but the charismatic gifts mentioned by St. Paul were rarely seen. One of the reasons for their decline may have been because the laity had no idea these gifts were in existence.[13]

---

10 McDonnell and Montague, *Christian Initiation and Baptism in the Holy Spirit*, 164.
11 Ibid. 176–179.
12 St. Augustine, *City of God, Book 2,* (New York: Doubleday, 1958), chapters 8–9. In the fifth century St. Augustine wrote about several miracles that he knew about.
13 McDonnell and Montague, *Christian Initiation and Baptism in the Holy Spirit*, 114.

As the charisms decreased among the laity, so did the enthusiasm that was seen in the early church. In longing for the days when charisms played a more dominant role St. John Chrysostom (c. 347–407) wrote, "The present church is like a woman who has fallen from her former prosperous days."[14]

In the fifth century, St. Augustine (354–430) listed the gifts of Isaiah 11:2–3 as the gifts of the Holy Spirit. Their purpose, as far as the laity was concerned, was more to help one grow in holiness and faith than to serve. This teaching may have been due to the church's emphasis on clergy and liturgy over the laity.

In any case, this continued to be the thinking of the Church to the twentieth century. There was one charismatic gift that continued to flourish throughout the Middle Ages (fifth to fifteenth century CE). It was called "jubilation." This will be covered more in the chapter on the word gifts.

---

14 Ibid. 288.

Questions for Thought and Discussion

1. What is the specific purpose of the gifts of the Holy Spirit in Isaiah 11:2–3?

2. What is the purpose of the gifts of the Holy Spirit that St. Paul mentions in his letters?

3. What are some possible gifts of the Holy Spirit not mentioned by St. Paul?

4. In John 14:12 Jesus tells us that we will do even greater works than his. What do you think he meant by this? What does this mean for you?

5. Have you ever experienced the power of the Holy Spirit flowing through you? Briefly describe this experience. How did this experience affect you?

"You were taught with your former manner of life, to put off your old self, which is being corrupted by its deceitful desires; to be made new in the attitude o your minds; and to put on the new self, created to be like God in righteousness and holiness."

-Ephesians 4:22-24 NIV

CHAPTER 4

The Church's Re-discovery of the Holy Spirit

The twentieth century was an era of many theological changes and surprises in the Roman Catholic Church. One of these was the Second Vatican Council which began on October 11, 1962.[15] A second surprise was the spontaneous generation of what came to be called the Catholic Charismatic Renewal.

What was surprising about these two events was their positive focus on the laity. This change was very different from what the Church's attitude toward the laity had been since the late Middle Ages, especially following the Council of Trent.[16]

For about five hundred years, the theological view of the Catholic Church was what Avery Dulles called *the "Institutional Model."*[17] What was important in this model

---

15 The Second Vatican Council was a meeting of the Church hierarchy lasting from 1962-1965. It was started by St. Pope John XXIII.
16 The Council of Trent was the Catholic Church's response to the Protestant Reformation in the sixteenth century.
17 More information about the institutional model of the Church can be found in chapter two of the book, *Models of the Church*, by Avery Dulles.

was the Church functioning as an institution. The active participants in this ecclesial machinery were the clergy and religious. They were responsible to teach, sanctify and govern, while the laity were responsible to be taught, to be sanctified, and to be governed.

An example of how the hierarchy viewed its relationship with the laity can be seen in this quote from Saint Pope Pius X:

> The Church is essentially an *unequal* society, that is, a society comprising two categories of persons, the Pastors, and the flock… So distinct are these categories that with the pastoral body only rests the necessary right and authority for promoting the end of the society and directing all its members toward that end; the one duty of the multitude is to allow themselves to be led, and, like a docile flock, to follow the Pastors.[18]

This view of the laity was to change with the Second Vatican Council. In the Decree on the Apostolate of Lay people we're told:

> The Holy Spirit sanctifies the People of God through the ministry and the sacraments. However, for the exercise of the apostolate he gives the faithful special gifts besides (cf. 1 Cor. 12:7) … From the reception of these charisms, even the most ordinary ones, there arises for each of the faithful the right and duty of exercising

---

18   Pope Pius X, *Vehementer Nos: On the French Law of Separation*, #8 (1906).

them in the Church and in the world for the good of men and the development of the Church, in exercising them in the freedom of the Holy Spirit who breathes where he wills" (Jn. 3:8).[19]

This new view focused on the power of the Holy Spirit working through the laity as well as the hierarchy, and it may have been a response to Pope John XXIII's initial prayer: "Renew your wonders in this our day as by a new Pentecost."[20]

In response to this new vision of the Church was the emergence of the Catholic Charismatic Renewal. This began on February 18, 1967, with some college students on a retreat at Duquesne University. They had been praying that the Holy Spirit would come to life within them in a totally new way. The result was that many of them received the *baptism in the Holy Spirit*.

> So, what is the baptism in the Holy Spirit?

The baptism in the Holy Spirit is God responding to our prayer to bring to life the power of the Holy Spirit that he has already given us. The baptism in the Holy Spirit (also called the release of the Holy Spirit) is an experience of a deepened awareness of God's presence and love, an openness to the charismatic gifts of the Holy

---

19 Austin Flannery, ed., *Vatican Council II, The Conciliar and Postconciliar Documents*. (Collegeville: Liturgical Press, 1996), 769.
20 Quote is from *Humanae Salutis*, the opening speech of the Second Vatican Council, December 25, 1961, #23.

Spirit,[21] a love of the scriptures, a love of the sacraments, an awareness of spiritual warfare, a desire to evangelize, and a love for the Church.[22]

Stemming from a multidenominational charismatic move of the Holy Spirit beginning in the 1950s and '60s,[23] the Catholic Charismatic Renewal was a response to the new vision of the Church wrought by the Second Vatican Council. If the people were to take on a more active role in the Catholic Church, it was only by the power of the Holy Spirit that they would be able to do so.

In an address given to leaders of the Charismatic Renewal on July 15, 2015, Pope Francis quoted Cardinal Joseph Suenens saying: "The first error that must be avoided is including the Charismatic Renewal in the category of a Movement. It is not a specific Movement; the

> The Charismatic Renewal is a current of grace, a renewing breath of the Spirit.

---

21 Included are the gifts of preaching, teaching, faith, healing, miracles, prophecy, the discernment of spirits, the gift of tongues and the interpretation of tongues. (See Romans 12: 6–8 and 1 Corinthians 12: 4–10 as examples.)

22 Patti Gallagher-Mansfield has a more detailed list of the effects of the baptism in the Holy Spirit in her book, *As by a New Pentecost*, p. 61.

23 Fr. Dennis Bennett, an Episcopalian priest, introduced the experience of baptism in the Holy Spirit to his congregation in Van Nuys, California. Although ousted by his congregation, his continued preaching and writing began a charismatic move in several mainstream denominations. See *Nine-O clock in the Morning*, by Dennis Bennett.

Renewal is . . . a current of grace, a renewing breath of the Spirit for all members of the Church, laity, religious, priests, and bishops. It is a challenge for us all."

Pope Francis also quoted the Cardinal as saying, "May the Charismatic Renewal disappear as such and be transformed into a Pentecostal grace for the whole Church: to be faithful to its origin, the river must lose itself in the ocean."[24] In other words, the experience of baptism in the Holy Spirit should not be identified with the Charismatic Renewal per se, but with the whole Church.[25] These statements by Cardinal Suenens were made in 1975.

Many years later, this is still the view of the leadership in the Catholic Charismatic Renewal. Everyone who has been baptized, and especially those who have been confirmed, should be experiencing a deepened (deepening) love for God, an awareness of the gifts of the Holy Spirit, and a desire to share their faith with others. This should be the normal Catholic/Christian experience.

On one level, this immersion of baptism of the Holy Spirit into normal Catholic life has already taken place. Many who had formerly been active in attending charismatic prayer meetings are now more involved with ministering in their own parishes.

---

[24] Pope Francis, address given to leaders of the Charismatic Renewal on July 15, 2015.
[25] Pope Francis is paraphrasing Cardinal Suenens. The exact quote can be found in Cardinal Suenens's book, *A New Pentecost?* pp. 111 and 113.

They received a spiritual awakening through baptism in the Holy Spirit to serve outside the charismatic prayer groups.

And, as many have discovered, the charismatic prayer meeting is not the only place people experience the baptism in the Holy Spirit. As we're told in John 3:8, "The wind (or the spirit) blows where it wills." An example of this is the ACTS retreat that was born in San Antonio, Texas in 1987.

Based on the Cursillo retreat, ACTS (an acronym for Adoration, Community, Theology, and Service) has enabled many participants to have an intimate awareness of God's love for them and his presence in their lives. Their experience sounds like baptism in the Holy Spirit.

One retreatant, Art Garcia, wrote:

> My initiation to ACTS made me feel the joy of fellowship, worshiping God as a group, emulating the Apostles. As I later served on team, facilitating the retreat, I saw the transformation of the retreatants as they came closer to the Lord. Some of them broken, alone, or searching, transformed themselves into men of faith with a life-long commitment to God. Through ACTS I have seen many lives change in a miraculous way.

Another retreatant from ACTS, Andrew Ortiz, wrote:

> I had been asked [to attend an ACTS retreat] for about four years. I refused. One day my friend asked me to

attend, and I said maybe. He took it as a yes and registered me and even came to pick me up. In attending the retreat, I learned more about God, the Holy Spirit, and our Catholic faith. The Holy Spirit shook me to the core. I have now been clean from drugs for five and a half years. My Catholic faith is now very strong.

Still another retreatant, Ethel Garcia, had the following experience:

Before attending an ACTS Retreat, I was trying to get closer to God, but I felt like I wasn't quite getting there. I know it is a lifetime process, but I guess I felt I wasn't worthy enough. During the ACTS Retreat, I really felt God reaching out to me and telling me he really loved me. I came out of the retreat finally feeling I was on the path God wanted me to be on. I not only felt closer to Him, but I also felt closer to my friends and family members. I feel more connection, love, and compassion for all human beings. I have a long way to go in my journey to Jesus, but I feel that through what I experienced in ACTS, I am on the right road, and with the help of the Holy Spirit, I will continue down that road.

These are examples from people I know, but it shows that the power of the Holy Spirit has transformed their lives as it had those in the Charismatic Renewal. In the same way, those in Cursillo, Antioch weekend, Search, and even a Life Teen weekend will attest to having had a similar experience.

The truth is that *"baptism in the Holy Spirit* is captive to no camp, whether liberal or conservative. Nor is it identified with any one movement, nor with one style of prayer, worship, or community. On the contrary. . . baptism in the Holy Spirit belongs to the Christian inheritance of all those sacramentally initiated into the Church."[26]

In addressing the International Conference on the Charismatic Renewal in the Catholic Church on May 19, 1975, Pope Paul VI said: "How then could this 'spiritual renewal' not be an 'opportunity' for the Church and for the world."[27] Cardinal Yves Congar, one of the chief architects of Vatican II, has called the Renewal, "a grace that God has given to the times that we are living in."[28]

In 1992 Saint Pope John Paul II said, "The emergence of the Renewal following the Second Vatican Council was a particular gift of the Holy Spirit to the Church."[29] It is my opinion that what these Church leaders are talking about is not the Catholic Charismatic Renewal itself, but baptism in the Holy Spirit.

---

26 Kilian McDonnell and George T. Montague, *Christian Initiation and Baptism in the Holy Spirit* (Collegeville: The Liturgical Press, 1994), 382.
27 Pope Paul VI, "To Participants of the 3rd International Convention of the Catholic Charismatic Renewal," (May 19, 1975), Vatican website.
28 Yves Congar, *I Believe in the Holy Spirit, Book 2* (New York: Herder Crossroad, 2005), 158.
29 Pope John Paul II, "Address of His Holiness John Paul II to the Council of the 'International Catholic Charismatic Renewal Office,'" (March 14, 1992), Vatican website.

In an address Pope Francis gave to leaders of the Catholic Charismatic Renewal on June 8, 2019, he said:

> You asked me to tell you what the Pope and the Church expect from… the entire Charismatic Renewal… I expect this movement… to share baptism in the Holy Spirit with everyone in the Church. It is the grace you have received. Share it! Don't keep it to yourselves! [30]

Even though the term *"baptism in the Holy spirit"* is associated with the Catholic Charismatic Renewal, it refers to an experience common to many different groups in the Catholic Church. This experience is often born within these groups because they provide a framework for it.

Groups like Cursillo and Acts do this through their retreats and seminars. In the Catholic Charismatic Renewal, it is done through a series of talks called Life in the Spirit Seminar. The Steubenville retreat weekend is successful in bringing this renewal to youth. There is a group called Alpha that is bringing people into a personal relationship with Jesus Christ through videos, discussion, and fellowship.

---

30 Pope Francis, "Address of His Holiness Pope Francis to Participants in the International Conference of Leaders of the Catholic Charismatic Renewal International Service-Charis," (June 8, 2019), Vatican website.

I'm sure other groups can make the same claim. Those who have had these spiritual experiences are hungering and thirsting to know God more, and there is more that God wants to give them through the gifts of the Holy Spirit!

Someone might ask why this experience of baptism in the Holy Spirit is not encouraged from the pulpit? It is taught from the pulpit. Whenever the priest or deacon delivers a homily about God's love, growing in a deeper relationship with God, and serving, they are inadvertently talking about baptism in the Holy Spirit.

There is the assumption the Holy Spirit is going to empower the congregation to follow through on the message given. When we receive the sacraments, we presume that the power of the Holy Spirit will awaken the grace to serve.

There is a reason RCIA participants are taught that they will receive the power of the Holy Spirit when they are confirmed. There is the belief that something is going to happen. Children from elementary grades up through high school learn about the power of the Holy Spirit. What is often not taught is the variety of the gifts of the Holy Spirit and their use in everyday life.

One final point is that the sacraments set a foundation for the experience of baptism in the Holy Spirit. It is through the grace of the sacraments that a hunger, and a thirst for more of God is created, causing a sensitivity to the Holy Spirit to work in us. But we need to receive the sacraments with the right disposition.[31] We have to want the power of God's grace when we receive the sacraments.

Receiving the sacraments in this way will create a hunger and a thirst to know God more. It is this unquenchable hunger for God that will draw someone to seek the power of the Holy Spirit. It is in this spiritual quest that we will discover the gifts God has given us.

---

31 See the *Constitution on the Sacred Liturgy,* #11.

CHAPTER 5
Discovering the Isaiah 11:2-3 Gifts

Wisdom, Understanding, Counsel, Fortitude, Knowledge, Piety, Fear of the Lord

The Catholic Church teaches that the seven gifts of the Holy Spirit are given to everyone at baptism. These are strengthened at confirmation, and the recipient can also grow in the charismatic gifts.

But everyone receives the seven gifts of the Holy Spirit because they increase our sensitivity to the guidance of the Holy Spirit. This will ultimately make us holy, and holiness is the goal of every follower of Jesus Christ. As Saint Pope John Paul 11 wrote in his apostolic letter, *Novo Millenio Ineuente:* "To ask catechumens: 'Do you wish to receive Baptism?' means at the same time to ask them: 'Do you wish to become holy?'" (#31)

The seven gifts of the Holy Spirit (sometimes called the holiness gifts) may not appear as exciting as some of the more miraculous charisms. They don't have the power, enthusiasm, and self-importance that miracles, healing, and prophecy might bring. Nonetheless, holiness is what our Church and the world need more today than any other gift of the Holy Spirit. We need the gifts of holiness to stamp out the worldview of secularism dominating our culture.

Secularism is the belief that faith and religion have little if any value at all. We can see this in the media, politics, and values shaping our culture today.

> What is secularism?

In light of Isaiah 5:20,[32] secularism calls evil good and good evil. We can see this with the acceptance of abortion, premarital sex, and the abhorrence of traditional Christian values. If anyone wants to "be cool" or culturally "with it," they will embrace the secular worldview.

The secular mentality has also infiltrated the Church in the form of individualism. This worldview says that if we disagree with the teachings of the Pope on doctrine or moral theology, then he's probably wrong. This same attitude caused Adam and Eve to eat the forbidden fruit. It's rebellion against authority and, ultimately, against God.

Our culture will be drawn away from secularism by giving people something better: Jesus Christ. And the only way our culture will be drawn to Jesus is if they see Jesus in us— that is, by our becoming holy. That is why we've been given

---

32 Isaiah 5:20: "Woe to those who call evil good and good evil, who put darkness for light and light for darkness, and put bitter for sweet and sweet for bitter."

the gifts of Isaiah 11:2-3. So, let's see what these holiness gifts of the Holy Spirit are.

The first is the gift of wisdom. Proverbs 9:10 tells us that "The beginning of wisdom is fear of the Lord" (NAB). The root of wisdom is loving God above all things. This is mentioned in scripture as the first and greatest commandment (Deuteronomy 6:4–7, Matthew 22:37, Mark 12:30). If we put God first in our lives, then we will want what he wants, and what God wants will always be for our good. It doesn't take a brilliant mind to understand that this is the beginning of wisdom.

> Wisdom helps us see things from God's perspective.

Through wisdom, God can help us put some priority in our lives. Is it more important for me to be on a multitude of church committees or to spend more time at home with my family? Is making more money worth the cost? Is getting my own way really that important?

I can offer a couple minor examples of wisdom in my own life. One day I was all stressed out about multiple things that had to be done. There was no peace. Suddenly it occurred to me that everything was going to be okay. Everything would all get done if I focused on doing one thing at a time. It felt as if God was infusing this thought into my mind. But did I learn from it?

On another occasion, I was worried about a project that wasn't coming together. Combating several moments of stress, I sensed God telling me to trust him, and it would all come together. This assurance from God did give me a great deal of peace, and everything did work out. God's perspective was that he wanted me to be at peace.

Wisdom is being able to look at the facts and discern the correct action to take. Not only is this gift helpful with making life decisions it's also useful in solving problems that can arise working in a committee. Wisdom asks where is God in this situation, and what would he have me, or us, do?

Another way wisdom can help is with making moral decisions. Living in a world surrounded by multiple voices vying for our allegiance, wisdom helps us discern the best voice to hear. Since we have been created by God and for God, the voice we want to listen to will give greater glory to God. It helps us listen to those voices glorifying God and filter out those that are not.

Wisdom gives us the ability to make that choice freely. The Church doesn't want us adhering to a moral code simply because they tell us it's the right thing to do. They want us to follow Church teaching because we know it to be the right thing to do.[33] This comes with the gift of Wisdom.

The second gift is understanding. This gift gives us an insight into what God is doing with us. We may be going

---

33 Pope Paul VI, *Gaudium et Spes,* #17 (December 7, 1985), Vatican website.

through a series of trials like Job, but we are aware that God knows what he's doing. We can also see God's hand in spiritual dryness. For a while, God's

> The gift of understanding can help us know who we are in God's eyes.

presence may have seemed to have always been with us when suddenly he's nowhere to be found.

The gift of Understanding lets us know that in times of dryness and trials God can be closer than ever before. Understanding can help us rejoice in our trials because we know that God is going to use them for our good (Romans 5:8, James 1:2-4.) The gift of understanding gives us the ability to have faith in what God is doing with us even though we may not have a clear picture of it.

Mother Teresa of Calcutta (1910-1997) often had to use this gift in her own spiritual life. In 1928 Agnes Bojaxhiu entered the Sisters of Loreto, a missionary Order in Ireland. It was here that she took the name Sister Mary Teresa. In 1929 she moved to Darjeeling, West Bengal, India to continue her formation, and on May 25 of 1931 she was sent to teach at a girl's school in Calcutta. She enjoyed teaching at the school and was very popular with the girls.

Nine years later, she made her final vows and became Mother Teresa.[34] Taking on this title with Final Profession was a custom of the Loreto nuns. In 1944, she became the

---

34 May 24, 1937.

school's principal. But it wasn't until September 10, 1946, that Mother Teresa began her true mission.

While riding on a train from Calcutta to Darjeeling, India, she received her mission to quench the thirst of Jesus. Jesus wanted her to leave the life that she loved at the girl's school and begin serving the poorest of the poor in Calcutta. It was from this inspiration that she founded the Missionary Sisters of Charity.

For about two years, she experienced tremendous visions, interior locutions,[35] and other consolations drawing her closer to union with God.[36] But it was also during those two years that she was painfully striving to get permission to leave the Loreto Sisters and begin her new Order. On August 8, 1948, she was finally given permission to begin the Missionaries of Charity.

Five years later, she started speaking to her spiritual director about an intense spiritual dryness. Having previously experienced tremendous spiritual consolations, she now had no awareness of God's presence other than by faith. Aside from momentary respites this would continue for the rest of her life.

---

35 An interior locution is hearing God's voice.
36 Union with God is the highest level of mystical prayer accompanied with ecstasy, visions, locutions, and other spiritual experiences.

In a letter to her spiritual director, she wrote, "The whole-time smiling-Sisters & people pass such remarks… Could they but know …how my cheerfulness is the cloak by which I cover the emptiness and misery."[37]

This was her spiritual life. Her exterior life, though, was extremely successful. Her Order was continually growing, she received numerous awards, and she was one of the most admired women in the world.

She may have needed this cross for God to work with her in this remarkable way. It may have been God's tool to keep her humble, like St. Paul's thorn in the flesh (2 Corinthians 12:6-7.) Whatever God's reason was for her spiritual dryness, it was the gift of Understanding that enabled her to persevere through the spiritual darkness she was experiencing.

In addition to helping us grow spiritually, we can use the gift of Understanding to help others find God in their spiritual darkness. Teachers can use it to help their students comprehend the teachings of the Church.

Apologists can use it to give a reason for the suffering and evil in the world. Parents can use it to reason with their teens, and young adults can use it to make moral decisions. There are many ways we can use the gift of understanding in everyday life.

---

[37] Kolodiejchuk, Brian. *Mother Teresa: Come Be My Light.* p. 187. © by the Mother Teresa Center, exclusive licensee throughout the world of the Missionaries of Charity for the works of Mother Teresa. Used with permission.

The third gift is Counsel. Through this gift, we know, almost by instinct, what God wants us to do. We know this because of the gift and through practice using this gift. As with any gift, our skill in using counsel is refined with increased practice.

> Through the gift of counsel we know, almost by instinct, the correct way to act in a given situation.

One way we can practice using this gift is by listening to God's counsel in prayer. This will give us a greater sensitivity to hear his voice. An example of someone using the gift of counsel is Dietrich Bonhoeffer.

Dietrich Bonhoeffer (1906-1945) was a German, Lutheran theologian arrested during World War 11 for speaking out against the Their Riech. When he was later discovered to have been a part of a plot to assassinate Adolph Hitler, he was sentenced to death. Although his involvement with the plot was limited, he was named as one of the conspirators on some documents.

Bonhoeffer's attitude toward his imprisonment was that he had a purpose for being there. He would have rather not been in prison, but since he was there, he wanted to make sure that he accomplished God's purpose. He was convinced that God would work with and through him no matter his situation. This brought him a general sense of peace, even among occasional bouts of depression.

Throughout his imprisonment, Bonhoeffer had a pleasant, cheerful disposition. Because of this, he was well-liked by everyone, including the guards. One of the guards had even hatched a plot to help him escape, but he declined because of the effect it would have on his family. So, Bonhoeffer remained in prison, ministering to the prisoners and many of the guards.

Bonhoeffer had hoped he would one day be set free. He was engaged to be married and was anxious to resume ministering in the church. But on April 9, 1943, he was executed. Just before the guards led Bonhoeffer to the gallows, he took a friend aside and said, "This is the end-for me the beginning of life." [38]

Dietrich Bonhoeffer could see God's purpose in his prison sentence through the gift of Counsel. He knew he was exactly where God wanted him for whatever God's purpose was. This sounds a lot like Mother Teresa's gift of Understanding, but the gifts often do interact with each other.

The question for us is, how do we know when it is the Holy Spirit speaking to us? This is a good question. We learn how to listen to the Holy Spirit by listening to him. When we pray, we often listen to ourselves more than God. If we want to get in touch with listening to the Holy Spirit, we need to spend time listening to God in silence. In psalm 46:10 or 11 (depending on the translation) we are told, "Be still and know that I am God!" (NAB)[39]

---

38 Bethge, Eberhard. *Dietrich Bonhoeffer: A Biography.* p. 927
39 We need to spend time silently listening to God in prayer. But CCC 2639 reminds us that "praise" is also important for listening to the Holy Spirit.

When we ask the Holy Spirit to speak to us, he will. We may sense his words coming to us from the depths of our hearts, or we may not. If nothing else, we are taking the time to listen. We can also practice listening to the Holy Spirit with Lectio Divina. This is a technique of reading a verse of scripture and listening to God speak to us through it [40]

Another way to practice listening to the Holy Spirit is to use the four cardinal virtues in daily life.[41] These are prudence, justice, fortitude, and temperance. These will be discussed in the next chapter.

The fourth holiness gift is **Fortitude.** Since we'll cover this in the next chapter on virtues, we'll go right into the fifth holiness gift, which is **knowledge.**

The gift of **Knowledge** is often confused with having a good memory. People are said to be knowledgeable if they can mentally retrieve large amounts of information. Someone like this will be said to be very knowledgeable, at least in a specific area. A doctor has this

> Knowledge is the ability to understand truths about our faith and God.

---

[40] Basically, there are four parts to Lectio Divina. 1: Read and reflect on what was read. 2: Read and imagine yourself in the scene. 3: Read and have a conversation with God. 4: Read and ask God what he expects of us. It's a little bit more detailed than this but it all involves listening.

[41] The Cardinal virtues are described in greater detail in CCC 1806, 1807, 1808, and 1809.

kind of knowledge in medicine, lawyers in law, mechanics in cars, and so on. This kind of knowledge is acquired by genetics and practice. It can be useful in applying the Gift of Knowledge, but it is not the gift itself.

The Gift of Knowledge is information about our faith and God that is revealed to us by God. More specifically, it is a growing knowledge of who we are, who God is, and what he expects of us. It may come slowly, suddenly like a flash of light, or both. Whatever way God sends this knowledge to us, its purpose is to draw us to holiness.

For instance, someone may know by faith that God loves them. It's what they've been taught, and they believe it. Suddenly they *know* God loves them. This knowledge may be the fruit of a retreat, an experience in prayer, or just because God wills it.

I had this experience while arguing with a friend in a restaurant. One moment we were arguing, and the next moment I was in tears, overwhelmed with the awareness of God's love. There's a big difference between believing someone is loved by God and knowing it.

But the gift of knowledge is not just an intense spiritual experience. When we receive the Holy Spirit at baptism and especially during Confirmation, the seeds of knowledge begin to take root in our souls. But we need to prepare our spiritual soil through prayer, reading scripture, spiritual reading, receiving the sacraments, etc., for the truths of our faith to become clearer to us.

Someone may believe by faith that Jesus is truly present in the Eucharist. Their parents taught them this, they heard it preached at Mass, and they may have even read about it on their own.

One day during Eucharistic adoration or after receiving Communion, they suddenly realize they *know* Jesus is present in the Eucharist. They have moved from merely believing this theological fact to knowing it in the depths of their heart. The book *201 Inspirational Stories of the Eucharist*, by Sister Patricia Proctor, OSC, is filled with testimonies of people who have had this experience.

Most people who pray believe that God is listening. They believe in faith that God is concerned for them and will answer their prayers. But sometimes, prayer is very dry, and it seems like they're just talking to the wind. God may occasionally withdraw the sensory awareness of his presence, giving us an opportunity to grow in faith. And sometimes, it takes almost every ounce of faith we have to believe we're getting through to God. Suddenly, we *know* God is present to us and listening to every word we say. We don't just believe it; we know it.

These experiences I've been talking about can be called *infused knowledge* because God directly imparts this awareness. But this gift is always present to those who have received the Holy Spirit. As we cooperate with God through prayer and study, our knowledge of God, ourselves and the credibility of Church teaching will increase. The purpose of these infused experiences is to add to our knowledge. They are placed in our memories and are a resource for us to turn to when more faith is required.

People can serve others with this gift by giving them hope. Their faith and trust in a God they *know* can be very contagious.

The sixth gift is piety. This gift enables us to be respectful of God and our Church. It is a sense that our relationship with God and the Church is important to us and should be for others.

> Piety shows respect for God and the Church.

When someone speaks respectfully about their faith, others are drawn to listen. They might even think, "What does this person know that I don't?" When someone visiting a church spots a parishioner actively involved with the liturgy and respectfully praying the Mass, they will be drawn to that.

One day my wife was able to plant some seeds in the heart of a little boy attending Mass with his mom. The little boy pointed to my wife and said, "Mom, that lady looks like she likes going to Mass." And then he said, "I don't like going to Mass." He would have rather been watching television or playing video games. Nonetheless, he will remember seeing someone who <u>really</u> looked like she enjoyed coming to Mass and it will get him thinking.

The gift of piety enables the recipient of this gift to evangelize. There are many ways we can use this gift as an evangelical tool. For instance, Catholics often make the sign of the cross while praying in a public place. It's no big deal, but God can use that act of piety to plant seeds of faith in someone's heart.

The seventh gift is fear of the Lord. This gift is an awareness of the awesomeness of God! Everything in the universe was created by God for us! All the laws of physics, the billions of galaxies, and the position of our planet in the solar system have been perfectly designed by God for us. And this God who created the entire universe, and has no beginning or end, loves each one of us personally. He is constantly present to us, thinking about us, and planning wonderous things for our lives.

In the commentary to his poem, *The Living Flame of Love,* St. John of the Cross reminds us "that if a person is seeking God, his beloved is seeking him much more." [42] We matter to God! We are important to him! How could we not want to shout out our praises to God! The seventh gift enables us to know just how awesome God truly is! And because of this, we have a fear of offending him. It's not so much a fear of being punished as a fear of offending such a wonderful, marvelous God. It is a call to obedience out of love.

---

42 Kieran Kavanaugh, OCD and Otillio Rodriguez, OCD, trans., *The Collected Works of St. John of the Cross.* (Washington, D.C.,: Institute of Carmelite Studies, 1979), 620.

An excellent example of someone with this gift was St. Ignatius Loyola. He was born with the name Iñigo Lopez de Oñaz de Loyola. He later changed his name to Ignatius after St. Ignatius of Antioch, whom he admired.

In his youth, he was caught up in the ways of the world, including gambling, womanizing, and swordplay. His goal in life was to be a valiant knight winning fame and the admiration of women.

In 1521 he was given the opportunity to turn his dream into reality. He was part of a small Spanish force sent to defend the town of Pampeluna from a much larger detachment of French soldiers. During his valiant effort, he was struck in the leg with a French cannonball, breaking one leg and wounding the other.

Convalescing in the Loyola castle, Ignatius underwent several painful operations, none of which gave him the desired result. He ended up with one leg shorter than the other and he walked with a limp for the rest of his life.

During his recovery, Iñigo grew bored and asked for a romance novel on chivalry to pass the time. The only books that could be found was one on the life of Christ and another on the lives of the saints.

He hesitantly accepted these but found they were just the books he wanted. The saints had the same chivalry and bravery he had admired in his romance novels. Whereas the heroes in his novels were fighting for an earthly lord, the saints were fighting for their Lord, Jesus Christ.

While reading about the saints, Iñigo began to wonder what it would be like to live as they did. Alternating with these thoughts was a scheme he was concocting on how to win the affection of a noble lady. After playing with these different thoughts for some time, he began to realize that the thoughts which gave him the greatest peace were those about spiritual things. He discerned the peace that came with them was God's voice speaking to him.

Shortly after that, he had a vision of the Blessed Mother holding the child Jesus. From this vision, the fear of the Lord, began to develop in St. Ignatius. He started doing great penances and mortifications solely to please Jesus. Ignatius grew in his desire to serve Jesus, and he tried to do it by emulating the lives of the saints. Although Ignatius's goal was to become more like the saints, this practice had an undesirable consequence.

In 1522 he was living as a layman in a Dominican Monastery, in Manresa earning his keep working at a hospital. He still had time to spend 7 hours a day in prayer, fasting and self-mortification in a nearby cave. It was at this time that he fell into a severe depression. He was overwhelmed with the thought that he had forgotten to confess something in his previous confession.

Even though he repeatedly confessed his sins to a priest, he could not overcome the feeling that he had forgotten to mention something. The depression and anxiety were so severe that Ignatius even considered taking his own life. It didn't seem like he would ever have any relief from this. Fortunately, he chose not to commit suicide because he knew it would displease the Lord.

Eventually, God did set him free from these scruples. As Ignatius journeyed through his experience of desolation, he learned how to guide souls through their own experience of darkness. Through this experience, Ignatius learned how to differentiate God's voice from the devil's.[43]

He learned that the devil could tempt someone to abuse the gift of Fear of the Lord. While it does draw someone to greater holiness, a lack of prudence can have devastating results. That's why it's vital for someone growing in this gift to have fellowship with mature Christians and a spiritual director.

The purpose of the seven gifts of the Holy Spirit in Isaiah 11:2–3 is to dispose us to the guidance and influence of the Holy Spirit, which will enable us to become holy. Everyone can benefit from using these gifts in their everyday life. Parents can benefit from the seven Isaiah gifts in daily family living.

---

43 St. Ignatius discusses scruples in #346-349 in the Spiritual Exercises. Basically, he says to do or believe the opposite of what the evil one is tempting.

Youth can benefit from daily decision-making, morality, and discovering the path that God has for them. Employers, employees, politicians, and religious leaders can all benefit from these "holiness" gifts of the Holy Spirit. They are a part of the gift of the Holy Spirit that we receive at baptism and confirmation.

What we need to do is start using them. It's like high-performance fuel in the engine of an expensive racecar. Nothing's going to happen until we turn the key in the ignition. We need to start using the gifts God has given us.

Questions for Thought and Discussion

1. What is secularism and why is it a problem for the church today?

2. The gift of wisdom can be described as "seeing things from God's perspective." How can this gift help you to live a holy life?

3. The gift of understanding gives us an insight into what God is doing with us. How can this gift help you to live a holy life?

4. The gift of counsel helps us to know, almost by instinct, the correct way to act in a given situation. How can this gift help you to live a holy life?

5. The gift of fortitude is the strength to live a Christian life. Name a situation where this gift can help you to live a holy life.

6. The gift of knowledge gives us the ability to understand truths about God. Name a situation where this gift can help you to live a holy life.

7. The gift of piety helps us to be respectful of God and the church. Name a situation where this gift can help you to live a holy life.

8. The fear of the Lord is the gift that helps us to be in awe of Almighty God. How can this gift help you to live a holy life?

"Rejoice always. Pray without ceasing. In all circumstances give thanks, for this is the will of God for you in Christ Jesus."

-1 Thessalonians 5:16-18- NAB

CHAPTER 6
Discovering the Cardinal Virtues

The four Cardinal Virtues are prudence, justice, fortitude, and temperance. Implementing these can help us listen to God because they require us to pause before taking action. You can use the paused time to pray about a situation and think it through.

Prudence is simply looking before you leap. It is weighing each situation's pros and cons and making the most reasonable choice. It is taking the time to think and pray before making a decision.

A good technique for prudence can be found in St. Ignatius of Loyola's rules for making a sound and good election. It can be tedious and takes some time to accomplish. Still, it will decrease the likelihood of making a later regretted decision.

The first part of this technique is to bring a Yes/No question to God. People might ask God if it's his will for them to get married, enter religious life, buy a car, change jobs, take a cruise, go back to school, or other decisions they might need to make. The discerner writes the request on the top of a sheet of paper, asking God to guide their decision.[44] Directly beneath the written request, they make two adjacent columns.

In one column, the discerner writes all the reasons why they should make their requested decision, and in the opposing column, all the reasons for not making that decision. If the pros outweigh the cons, the discerner continues to pray about the decision.[45]

It's important to note that for this to work, one must want God's will more than anything else. The result of this will be what's called *Ignatian Indifference*.[46] For instance, Smitty has asked Sarah to marry him. There is a part of Sarah that would like to marry Smitty, but what she wants even more is to do God's will. Sarah has Ignatian Indifference. It's easy to see how it might take a lot of prayer and reflection to reach this point.

It's helpful to have a good co-discerner on hand. A co-discerner knows spiritual things, is trusted by the discerner, and is indifferent to the outcome. Their job is to help the discerner differentiate God's voice from their own and others.

The discerner can then make a list of alternatives to the original request.[47] For instance, some alternatives to marriage

---

44 The Spiritual Exercises of St. Ignatius #178 and #180.
45 Ibid. 181.
46 Ibid. #179.
47 Ibid. #182.

might be entering religious life, working on an advanced degree, pursuing a career, maintaining a current state of independence, and so on. Does the discerner's desire for any of these outweigh their desire for marriage? Will any of the alternatives enable the discerner to serve God better? For each of the alternatives, pros and cons are listed. A third list can also be made exploring how this decision will affect their family and those closest to them.

This exercise in discernment will help the discerner discover what they truly want in life and what God wants for them. After exploring and praying about the pros and cons, the alternatives, and their effect on others, the discerner reflects on which option gives him the greatest peace. The experience of peace will give greater clarity on the road that should be traveled.

For those without the time or patience to go through this process, it is still good to weigh the pros and cons, look at alternatives, pray, and take some time listening to the Lord's response. Sales personnel will usually not want to make deals in this way. Their goal is to make someone so enthusiastic about making a purchase they think only with their emotions.

One principal point of discernment is that it's never good to make a decision when our emotions are either at their peak or in a deep valley. The best time for making a choice is when we're completely at peace. Prudence is a gift of the Holy Spirit that helps us make wise decisions. The only way it can come to life, though, is by our using it.

The virtue of **Justice** lives out the two greatest commandments: love God first and love your neighbor as yourself. The irony in this virtue is that one cannot love God without loving one's neighbor.[48] Therefore, if we keep from others something that rightly belongs to them, we're keeping this from God as well. We are stealing it from him because, ultimately, everything belongs to God.

The Catechism of the Catholic Church tells us: "In his use of things man should regard the external goods he legitimately owns not merely as exclusive to himself but common to others also" (CCC 2404.) This rule is in the section dealing with the seventh commandment: "You shall not steal."[49]

We need to provide the basic living needs for those who cannot care for themselves because it is rightfully theirs (CCC 2446.) Practicing the virtue of justice invites us to prayerfully reflect on our obedience to follow Jesus's command to love our neighbor. It helps us practice listening to God in that we have to consciously make a choice for justice.

We can learn a lesson about justice from some eighth-century BCE prophets. At this time, the nations of Judah and Israel were experiencing tremendous economic prosperity. Their united wealth could've been an opportunity for everyone to unite in thanking God for his abundant blessings. What emerged from this, though, was a super-wealthy

---

48 "If anyone says, 'I love God,' but hates his brother, he is a liar." (1 John 4:20)
49 The section on the seventh commandment is in CCC 2401–2449.

and a super-poor class of people. The wealthy were the merchants and government officials, while the poor were primarily farmers.

In their greed to make even more money, the merchants overcharged the farmers for their needed supplies. When they borrowed money to pay for these items, they were given an elevated interest rate, prohibiting them from ever getting out of debt. The debtors confiscated their property, leaving them with nothing.

Those who were ripping off the poor farmers saw nothing wrong with this at all. They continued to worship God, keeping all the festivals and rites of their faith. They believed they were still in God's good graces as long as they kept the ritualistic ordinances of their faith.

But the prophets spoke vehemently against this corruption. Among them were Hosea, Amos, Micah, and the prophet of third Isaiah. The message they gave can be summarized in this passage from Amos 5:21-24:

> "I hate, I despise your feasts, I take no pleasure in your solemnities. Even though you bring me your burnt offerings and grain offerings I will not accept them. Your stall-fed communion offerings I will not look upon them. Take away from me your noisy songs; The melodies of your harps, I will not listen to them. Rather, let justice surge like waters and righteousness like an unfailing stream" (NAB).

Injustice still exists in our world today. One of the greatest is abortion because it denies someone a right to life. Catholics and all Christians need to be actively involved in eliminating this and all forms of injustice. As we learn from the prophets, our spiritual practices are meaningless if they're not coupled with justice.

Taking the time to consider others' needs and what our response should be help us practice listening to God's voice.

Fortitude or courage gives us the grace to say "No" to temptations to sin, "Yes" to sharing our faith with others, and "Yes" to living by our moral values. St. James gave a good maxim for this when he wrote, "Be doers of the word and not hearers only, deluding yourselves" (James 1:22, NAB).

Fortitude says that we not only talk the talk but also walk the walk. It gives us the courage to be an authentic disciple of Jesus Christ. The virtue of courage, which is also a gift, calls us to seek God's strength whenever we're afraid.

When I think of the virtue of fortitude, I'm reminded of the ministry of David Wilkerson (1931-2011).[50] In 1958, he was an Assembly of God minister in Philipsburg, Pennsylvania. One evening as he was praying, his eyes ran across a story in Life magazine about seven teenage boys

---

50 David Wilkerson's story can be read about in the book *the Cross and the Switchblade,* by David Wilkerson and John and Elizabeth Sherrill.

in New York City. They were all convicted of murder. He sensed God telling him to go to New York and minister to those kids.

His first attempt to do so was a complete failure. In trying to get the judge's attention, he was rushed out of the courtroom by security, questioned by the media, and his picture made national headlines. This exposure gave him the reputation of being a crazy preacher, and even those in his own denomination criticized him.

He was initially discouraged by his apparent failure. Maybe he had mistaken his own voice for God's. But as he continued to pray, the desire to return to New York City kept coming back to him.

When he got to New York this second time, he was recognized by a small-time gang as the preacher who had the run-in with the police at the trial. What had previously appeared to be a mistake gave him some clout with the gang and opened the door for him to meet other gangs. Some welcomed him, and others didn't want anything to do with him. But despite any fear he may have sensed, he continued sharing his message with the gangs that God loved them.

He eventually held a city-wide youth rally inviting all of New York City's gangs. Initially, it didn't seem like the crusade was having much of an effect on the gangs. On the last night, though, several gang members gave their lives to Jesus Christ.

Eventually, this started Teen Challenge, which has become Adult and Teen Challenge. This is a worldwide ministry whose goal is to help adults and teens find freedom from self-destructive behaviors. Their solution is a personal relationship with Jesus Christ.

None of this would have ever happened without David Wilkerson courageously responding to God's call. Any fear David encountered was replaced with the awareness that God was with him. The virtue of fortitude can work with us in the same way.

God's courage will take over when we walk in the way he calls us, despite rejection, persecution, or physical harm. But we need to start using this gift to bring it to life. Practicing the virtue of fortitude is another way of learning how to listen to God's voice.

Temperance is the virtue that strives to live in moderation. We naturally move towards that which gives us the greatest pleasure and satisfaction. This quest for satisfaction can be a good thing when it motivates us to improve ourselves and others. However, the desire for pleasure can cause us to abuse ourselves, others, and the material goods God has given us.

The virtue of temperance gives us a respect for and appropriate use of God's creation. It enables us to give glory to God for the gift rather than glorifying ourselves in the gift. We can easily find examples that show how intemperate behavior can abuse God's gifts.

In 1 Corinthians 14:27-33, Paul addressed an abuse of the gifts of tongues and prophecy. He encouraged their use but wanted it done in order and with love. Some Corinthians used these gifts anytime they wanted, disrupting their worship service. Paul told them these gifts were under their control and should be done in order because we have a God of peace.

Another one of God's gifts is wine. Psalm 104:15 tells us that God gives us wine to gladden our hearts. In 1 Timothy 5:23, Paul says, "Stop drinking only water, but have a little wine for the sake of your stomach and your frequent illnesses" (NAB). But Paul also says, "And do not get drunk on wine, in which lies debauchery, but be filled with the Spirit" (Ephesians 5:18). The conclusion is there's nothing wrong with drinking wine as long as it's done in moderation.

Another example is eating. In the Gospels, Jesus was frequently eating with people. He provided food for the multitude,[51] asked the apostles to give him something to eat [52] and even ate breakfast with them.[53] The blessing of food and the gift of taste are wonderful gifts of God. Still, the gift of food can be misused. Overeating can cause harm to our bodies and can be a replacement for going to God with our problems.

---

51 Matthew 14:13-21, Mark 6:31-44, Luke 9:12-17 and John 6:1-14
52 Luke 24:42
53 John 21:12

Another example of intemperance is spiritual gluttony. Seeking God is often accompanied by feelings of great peace and joy. These initial gifts are good because they motivate us to continue on our spiritual journey.

However, people can become so used to these positive feelings that they crave them more than God. Unconsciously, they might even start worshipping these feelings rather than Almighty God. And when God starts to remove these feelings so they can grow in faith, they feel like God has abandoned them. They get discouraged, and if they're not careful, they can leave God altogether.

We can receive many blessings from the virtue of temperance and all the virtues. Their purpose is to slow us down, give us time to listen to God, and follow his lead.

Questions for Thought and Discussion

The Cardinal Virtues

1. Describe a situation where you could use the virtue of Prudence in your life.

2. Would the discernment technique mentioned be helpful in this situation?

3. Can you think of another situation where this technique would be helpful?

4. How can you apply the virtue of Justice to your own life?

5. Can you give examples of injustice in the world today? What are some ways you can make these situations more just?

6. How do you see the virtue of Temperance in your life? Are there ways you could apply this virtue more?

7. How do you see the virtue of Fortitude in someone you admire? Where in your life would you like to see more of this virtue?

8. How could these virtues be helpful in promoting the gift of Counsel?

CHAPTER 7
Discovering the Word Gifts

Tongues, Interpretation of Tongues, and Teaching

The gift of tongues is probably the most misunderstood gift of the Holy Spirit. Many Catholics are afraid or at least concerned about it because it hasn't been a part of their normal Catholic experience. And yet, Catholics in the Middle Ages would have had no problem with the gift of tongues.

At the time it was thought to be a real language enabling evangelists to preach in foreign lands.[54]

The gift of tongues that still existed as a form of praise was now called "jubilation." St. Jerome (347–402 CE) wrote: "By the term 'jubilus' we understand that which neither in words nor syllables or letters nor speech is it possible to express or comprehend how much man ought to praise God"[55]

---

[54] McDonnell and Montague, *Christian Initiation and Baptism in the Holy Spirit*, 366.
[55] Quoted in *Sounds of Wonder: A Popular History of Speaking in Tongues in the Catholic Tradition, by* Eddie Ensley (New York/Ramsey: Paulist Press, 1977), 8.

In Romans 8:26, St. Paul mentions our inability to express ourselves in prayer. He writes that "the Spirit too comes to the aid of our weakness; for we do not know how to pray as we ought, but the Spirit himself intercedes with inexpressible groanings" (NAB). These "groanings" sound like what St. Jerome was referring to and what today is called the gift of tongues.

St. John Chrysostom (347–407) wrote: "It is permitted to sing songs without words as long as the mind is focused on God."[56] In the sixth century, Pope Gregory the Great (540–604) wrote: "By the term "jubilation" we mean a joy of the heart that cannot be expressed in speech, yet the person who is rejoicing makes this joy known in certain ways—this joy cannot be concealed, yet cannot be fully expressed (in words)."[57]

Pope Gregory also wrote: "Let angels therefore praise because they know such brightness; but let men who are limited by speech jubilate."[58] St. Augustine (354–430) wrote:

> What is jubilation? Joy that cannot be expressed in words. Yet the voice expresses what is conceived in the heart and cannot be expressed in words. This is jubilation. [59]

St. Teresa of Avila (1515–1582) also shared about jubilation. In her book *The Interior Castle,* she wrote:

---

56 Quoted in *Sounds of Wonder: Speaking in Tongues in the Catholic Tradition* by Eddie Ensley. 9
57 Ibid..17
58 Ibid. 17.
59 Ibid, 8.

> Our Lord sometimes gives the soul feelings of jubilation and a strange prayer it doesn't comprehend ... What I'm saying seems like gibberish, but certainly the experience takes place in this way, for the joy is so excessive the soul wouldn't want to enjoy it alone but wants to tell everyone about it so that they might help this soul praise the Lord.[60]

There are several examples that could be given to show the use of jubilation among the saints. These few have been presented to show that the experience is not foreign to Catholic tradition. While it could be argued that the saints did not view jubilation as the gift of tongues, their description of it sounds identical to what St. Paul was talking about in Romans 8:26. The primary purpose of the gift of tongues is for praise.

When we run out of words to praise God in our own language, there's the gift of tongues. And as we continue to praise God with the gift of tongues, they will often become silent as we enter into a more quiet and contemplative adoration.

> **When words are not enough to convey the level of praise that is intended, there is the gift of tongues.**

Some people say they used to pray in tongues, but now they're drawn to contemplative prayer. There doesn't need

---

60 Kieran Kavanaugh OCD and Otilio Rodriguez OCD, trans., *The Collected Works of St. Teresa of Avila, Vol. 2.* (Washington, D.C.: Institute of Carmelite Studies, 1980), 395.

to be a discrepancy at all. Praying in tongues can lead into a quieter state of adoration and contemplation.

We can praise God in tongues whenever and wherever we want to. When we're in a situation where our praying in tongues might be offensive to someone, we can pray in tongues mentally. This is a great help when we're taking an exam or in a stressful situation. When I pray in tongues, even if it is done mentally, I can sense the power of the Holy Spirit praying through me.

The gift of tongues is a vocal expression of what the Holy Spirit is praying in the believer's heart. But it is a language that is unknown to the person speaking it. There have been cases where the words spoken were understood as a specific language, but this will usually not be the case. Because of this, it is often argued that the gift of tongues is nothing more than nonsensical gibberish.

This may be the case. But in 2009, the Linguistic Society of America determined there to be 6,909 known languages.[61] Many languages have since died out, and God can invent a language at will. So, just because the meaning of the sounds being emitted is not understood by the people listening does not mean that someone's gift of tongues isn't an actual language.

---

61 My source for this is https://www.linguisticsociety.org/content/how-many-languages-arethere-world.

But even if the gift of tongues is nonsensical gibberish, "The Lord looks into the heart" (1 Samuel 16:7). The Lord knows what's in someone's heart, whether it's gibberish, a forgotten language, or just one that is unknown to the listeners.

Another purpose for the gift of tongues is praying for others. If we're praying with someone for healing, we may not know what their need is. But the Holy Spirit does. Suppose the person we're praying with is not familiar with this gift, and we're concerned about offending them. In that case, we can pray in tongues silently. When we're praying in tongues with someone, we're praying in faith that the Holy Spirit knows their need.

It is true, of course, that we don't have to use tongues when praying for someone. The Holy Spirit knows the need, whether we pray in tongues or not. One advantage of praying in tongues is that it enables us to minister more. We can pray, "Lord, meet their need. Thy will be done. Heal them from whatever is causing their pain," and then it's all over.

When we pray in tongues, though, we can minister to them longer because we don't have to worry about running out of words. The recipient often feels a grand sense of peace when prayed for in tongues.

Another use of the gift of tongues is what St. Paul calls the interpretation of tongues. During a charismatic prayer meeting someone will receive a sense to pray in tongues. Afterward, the interpretation of that tongue will be spoken, either by the speaker or someone else, in the common language. It is not a direct translation but more the gist of what was said. How do we know if the message given is from the Lord? Every presumed message from God needs to be spiritually discerned (1 John 4:1.)

When someone asks God to receive the gift of tongues it might come immediately or not for some time. Why this happens, God only knows. But it has absolutely nothing to do with the level of God's love for them or their holiness. God works with everyone in the way and in the time that is best for them.

Sometimes God will grant someone the gift of tongues, and they don't know how to open up to it. One remedy is to start talking gibberish or baby talk. Talking gibberish will at least get the tongue to start moving. As the worshiper praises God, they will notice their speech becoming more articulate. As the sounds flow fluently from their lips, they will sense the Holy Spirit praying through them.

Are there arguments against praying in tongues? Of course, there are. But it is one of the gifts of the Holy Spirit mentioned by St. Paul. It has been a part of the Catholic experience, and many Catholics today pray in tongues. Furthermore, it is mentioned as a viable gift in the Catechism of the Catholic Church (CCC 2003). There's no reason for anyone to fear or be concerned about its validity.

The Gift of Teaching

I like to call the gift of tongues and the interpretation of tongues "word gifts" because they minister through the spoken word. I want to also include with the word gifts the charism of "teaching."

The teacher is someone who can express their faith in a way that gives encouragement and instruction to others. This gift can be used in speaking at conferences, giving retreats, teaching a catechism class, preaching, and so on. It can also be used in sharing our faith with others.

The purpose of this gift is to enable the listener to hear the Holy Spirit's voice. If all the listeners comes away with is admiration for the teacher's skill, the teacher has not done their job.

> The purpose of the gift of teaching is to enable the listener to hear the Holy Spirit speaking to them through the teacher's words.

There's an old story about a trained actor who recited the twenty-third psalm at a church fiesta. The people whistled, applauded, and cheered after his presentation.

But then an older man in the audience walked up to the podium, recited the twenty-third psalm, and sat down.

Silent awe came over the people when the older man finished reciting the psalm, bringing some to tears. The professional actor went up to the podium again and said, "The difference in our presentations is that I know the psalm; the old man knows the shepherd."

In the same way, we should not be drawn to the teacher's eloquence but to the simplicity of the Holy Spirit speaking to us. The purpose of the teacher is to clean out our spiritual ears, enabling us to hear the Holy Spirit's voice. So, it is not necessary for a teacher to be a scholar, have an advanced degree in theology, or even a high I.Q. A teacher is someone who has an advanced love for God and the desire to share their faith with others.

It is important to remember the gift of teaching comes from God, and a natural gift of teaching comes from the intellect. They are two different things. Someone can have both, of course, but the gift of teaching can also come to someone without the genetic predisposition. They may find it challenging to teach initially, but as their focus becomes less on themselves and more on God, it will become easier for them.

I am saying that if someone is hungry to share their faith through teaching, they should do it. It is only in this way they will discover whether they have a gift for it or not. The real test will come with the response they get from their listeners. Teachers must ask themselves whether the listeners are drawn more to God or their presentation.

One final point on teaching. In *Evangeli Nuntiandi #41*, Pope Paul V1 says "Modern man listens more willingly to witnesses than to teachers, and if he does listen to teachers, it is because they are witnesses." Even if one has the gift of teaching, their words will be more effective if coupled with firsthand experience.

Personal testimony and true stories are very compelling for this.

Questions for Thought and Discussion

The Word Gifts

1. What are some ways the gift of tongues can be used in everyday life?

2. How could the interpretation of tongues be used in everyday life?

3. What problems might an intelligent person have with the gift of teaching?

4. What attributes should a good teacher have?

5. Why do you think praying in tongues is not necessarily a sign of holiness?

6. How could you use the interpretation of tongues outside of a charismatic prayer meeting?

7. Do you think the gift of tongues is a real language? Can you justify your answer?

"Now I should like all of you to Speak in tongues, but even more to prophecy."

-1 Corinthians 14:5-NAB

CHAPTER 8
Discovering the Gifts of Power:

Healing and Miracles

Healing and the working of miracles are both gifts of the Holy Spirit. The New American Bible calls miracles "mighty deeds," but it means the same thing. A miracle is an extraordinary event that the laws of nature or science cannot explain. It is the same with miraculous healing. There is no scientific reason why healing should have taken place, but it did.

For instance, there are several examples of miraculous healings that have been documented taking place from the waters of Lourdes. One of the first Lourdes miracles took place with a two-year-old boy named Justin Bouhort in 1858. He had been very sick from birth, was unable to walk, and his prognosis was that he would not improve.

In desperation, his mother lifted her son and carried him to the spring at Massabielle. She prayed before the grotto and then lowered her son into the spring, keeping him there for some time. She then lifted him and returned home. That night Justin slept peacefully, and in the morning, it was obvious his condition had improved.

Justin quickly recovered and soon began to walk. He lived a long life and was even able to attend St. Bernadette's canonization in 1923. The doctor who had been treating him, Dr. Dozous, documented that Justin's healing could only be attributed to a miraculous intervention.[62]

A similar situation occurred with a friend of mine, Deacon Frank Smith. In 1996 he was diagnosed with bladder cancer. He received surgery to have it removed, but it returned. Frank continued to have the cancer removed only to have it return again for the next nine years.

By 2005 the cancer was progressing rapidly, and he needed another surgery immediately. Just before the surgery, though, Deacon Frank went to Lourdes to bathe in the miraculous waters. Shortly after returning from Lourdes, he went to the hospital for his scheduled surgery. When he woke up from the anesthesia, he was told they couldn't find any cancer.[63] The only explanation for his healing was that God had miraculously healed him from the water at Lourdes. So, miraculous healings still do take place.

There are also times when God works within natural law to heal. For instance, God expects us to go to the doctor when we get sick. After all, scripture tells us the doctor receives his

---

62 The information about Justin Bouhort was obtained from the website: http://www.miraclehunter.com/marian_apparitions/approved_apparitions/lourdes/miracles1.html.
63 This story was told to me by Deacon Frank Smith. He has given permission to tell his story here.

wisdom for healing from God.[64] If God wills to heal someone in a supernatural (or miraculous) way, it is entirely up to him, but we should never presume to know the mind of God.

Several years ago, my wife knew a lady who stopped taking the medicine the doctors had given her for stomach cancer. She did this to give proof of her faith in God. She eventually died. She might have died even if she had continued taking the medication, but she should not have given up one of God's means of bringing about her healing. Using the wisdom God has given doctors to heal us is not showing a lack of faith in God; it is how we show our faith in God.

There are, of course, miraculous healings that still do take place. When I was seven years old, I was in an automobile accident in Los Angeles, California. The doctors at the first hospital I was taken to said I would probably die, and there was nothing more they could do. My parents then took me to Children's Hospital in Hollywood. Their prognosis was pretty much the same, except they would do everything they could while I was still alive.

One day my mom asked the neurosurgeon what my prognosis was. He told her if I ever did regain consciousness, I would be severely handicapped, requiring institutionalization for the rest of my life. She went to our parish church (St. Bruno's in Whittier) and surrendered my life to God. When she returned

---

64 The book of Sirach 38:2 (this is also called the book of Ecclesiasticus).

to the hospital, she discovered that I had just regained consciousness following a nine-day coma. Three months later, I was out of the hospital, walking and preparing to return to school.

When my mom thanked the neurosurgeon for all he had done he said, "Don't thank me, thank God." Undoubtedly, the doctors' treatment and care added to my healing, but there was a certain point even the doctors knew was beyond their natural science.

My friend, Vince Montoya, does have a gift of healing, and he has seen many miraculous cures through his ministry. He discovered this gift in 1972 while praying with people at a Catholic charismatic prayer meeting. Since then, he has witnessed many miracles through his gift of healing.

In one case, Vince was teaching at a church when he suddenly felt led to stop. He walked over to a woman in the church and asked if he could pray with her. He later found out this lady was supposed to die. This was in 1995, and she is still alive today! Another lady had a lump in her eye. After he prayed with her, he said, "Where was the lump?" She reached where the lump had been, and it was now gone. One lady was rushed to the hospital from a heart attack. When Vince prayed with her in the hospital, she was immediately healed of her heart condition.

Not everyone has this gift, but God can work through anyone who asks him to bring healing to someone. But there is no way we'll know if we have this gift unless we're willing to pray with people. When someone tells us about an ailment they're having, whether it be physical, psychological, or spiritual, we need to ask if we can pray for them. It's OK to remember their need in personal prayer, but we minister more to the whole person when we pray *with* them.

God can instantaneously work miracles from heaven, but his preferred method is to work through us.[65] Scripture tells us that God used the pagan ruler, King Nebuchadnezzar, to purify the hearts of his people.[66] We're told that God sent another pagan, Cyrus the Great, to set his people free from their Babylonian captivity. God can work through and with whomever he wills. So, why wouldn't God use a doctor or us to assist him in bringing healing to someone?

I learned this when I prayed for my pastor for a healing from cancer. I sincerely believed God was going to miraculously heal him. When I asked about his condition the next day, he said he felt worse than the day before. I prayed with him once a week for three weeks with the same results. I began to think that maybe my prayers just weren't powerful enough to reach the ears of the Almighty. Afterward, he received medical treatment, and today he is cancer free.

His healing was good news, but why didn't God answer my prayer? All I know is that God didn't answer my prayer in the way or the time that I wanted him to. However, my

---

65 The purpose of the gifts of the Holy Spirit is for God to minister through us; see Romans 12:4–8 and 1 Corinthians 12:4–10.
66 Jeremiah 18:13–17, 21:1–14, 2 Chronicles 36:22–23.

pastor didn't experience any pain or discomfort often associated with radiation therapy. Perhaps that was a part of God's answer to my prayer. It may be that his healing was more rapid or more complete than it otherwise would have been.

God only knows how he answered my prayer. But we are told in scripture that God does answer prayer.[67] It may not be in our preferred way or time, but that's as it should be because he is God, and we are not. That's why 1 Thessalonians 5:18 encourages us to give thanks to God "In all circumstances . . . for this is the will of God for [us] in Christ Jesus."

But supernatural healing isn't the only way miracles can come to us. In the case of healing, God provides health where there once was suffering. Besides healing, there are other ways God has provided for the needs of his people. One rather famous incident occurred with Fr. Rick Thomas, S.J., and his prayer group in El Paso, Texas.

> Miracles can be defined as God providing something that wasn't there before.

On Christmas day in 1972, the prayer group brought food to feed the people who usually ate from the dump in Juarez, Mexico. They immediately could tell there would be a problem because they had only brought enough food to feed 120 people, and 300 people showed up. What were they going to do once they ran out of food?

---

67   See Matthew 18:19–20, 21:22, 7:7, Mark 11:24, Luke 11:9–13.

So, they kept serving, and they kept trusting. When they finished serving the 300 people, they still had enough food to donate to a local orphanage.[68] You can find several stories like this in the book, *Loaves and Fishes: Jesus and the Feeding of the Multitudes,* by Joseph D. Cieszinski. The stories in Joe's book show that God still does perform miracles.

One way we can receive a miracle in life is by asking God to provide one for us and believing that he will do it. Of course, God isn't going to perform some magic trick just to impress us. He doesn't need to do that. But if there is a need, we can pray for it and believe God has heard and will answer our prayer. However, we need to believe that the miracle will occur in God's way and time, not ours.

Sometimes God will answer our prayer by calling us to do our part. Several years ago, my wife and I volunteered for a radio program called *Albuquerque Alive.* Our job was to record testimonies over the phone and edit them into brief segments for airplay.

In one testimony, a lady shared how God had met their financial need. They had been praying for a miracle when a little boy came to their door one day and gave them a bag with money in it. It was the exact amount they had been praying for. This story sounded a little too miraculous to us, but maybe some people from their church had sent the little boy to give them the gift anonymously.

---

68 Joseph D. Cieszinski, *Loaves and Fishes: Jesus and the Feeding of the Multitudes,* (Goleta: Queenship, 2016), 48–52.

This testimony caught my attention because we were struggling financially. So, I began to pray, "God, why don't you send a little boy to our door with a bag full of money?" The answer he gave me was, "Why don't you go back to school so you can get a better-paying job?"

I didn't know how I could swing that financially, but God worked it out for me. I was able to go to school and eventually graduated with a master's degree in special education. Sometimes God will give us the miracle we ask for, but he wants us to participate with him in getting it.

If we take the time to think and pray about it, we can probably find many miracles that God has worked in our lives. But what about those miracles or healings that never happened? Some people might become angry with God when a loved one they've been praying for dies. They might wonder why God miraculously heals some people and not others. That's a very good question.

The only answer that can be given is a difficult one to accept: *God knows what he's doing.* In Isaiah 55:8–9 God tells us:

> For my thoughts are not your
> Thoughts,
> nor are your ways my ways
> (says the Lord).[69]

---

69 The translation in the New American Bible says, "Oracle of the Lord."

> For as the heavens are higher
> than the earth,
> so are my ways higher than
> your ways,
> My thoughts higher than
> your thoughts.

It's never an easy thing watching someone we love die. But it may help to view it from the deceased person's perspective. They're not the lifeless body we see lying in the coffin or the urn of ashes sitting on a table. They are alive in God's presence, and they are experiencing firsthand just how incredibly loved they are by Almighty God! It is an experience of complete acceptance and complete joy![70]

This reflection won't remove the pain of mourning, but it might give some meaning to a loved one's passing. There are many kinds of miracles for which we could be praying: a good job, a spouse, the conversion of a family member, a terminal illness, success in life, money to pay the bills, and many other requests that we might present to God. Whatever our request is, our prayer should always end with the phrase: "Yet not my will, but yours be done" (Luke 22:42).

Nonetheless, our job as Christians is to remind others that miracles are possible. We can do this by praying with

---

[70] "He will wipe every tear from their eyes, and there will be no more death or mourning, wailing or pain, [for] the old order has passed away" (Revelation 21:4).

them for the miracle, believing the miracle will take place, and helping them to see the miracle when it happens. Our support is especially crucial when the miracle has taken place other than how it was expected.

Questions for Thought and Discussion

Discovering the Gifts of Power

1. Recall a miracle that happened with you or with someone else. What does this tell you about God's love?

2. Do you think miracles occur as frequently today as in the early Church? Can you give an explanation for your answer?

3. Do you think we should be able to perform miracles similar to those Jesus did? Why, or why not?

4. What are some miracles we should be able to see in everyday life?

5. Why do you think God would grant a miraculous healing to one person and not to someone else?

6. How would you respond to someone who asked you why God didn't grant them the healing or the miracle they asked for? You want to give them facts and comfort.

"For we are his workmanship, created in Christ Jesus for good works, which God prepared beforehand, that we should walk in them."

-Ephesians 2:10'RSV

CHAPTER 9
Discovering the Gifts of Revelation

Prophecy, Word of Knowledge, Mental Images, and Discernment of Spirits

There's an old story about St. Joan of Arc composed partially of facts and partially of legend. The fact part of the story is that during the early fifteenth century, England and France fought with each other in what would later be called the Hundred Years' War.

France wasn't doing well in the struggle until a sixteen-year-old girl, Joan of Arc, began sharing her visions about a French victory. She convinced King Charles VI that her visions were authentic, so he gave her permission to lead his army against the English. Following several victories led by the young saint, the French morale increased, leading to their victory over the English.

The legend part is that one day Joan was telling King Charles about some things the Lord had told her when the king suddenly cried out, "Joan, you're constantly telling me about these messages God is giving you! How come he never talks to me? I am, after all, the king of France!" Joan said, "He is talking to you. You're just not listening."

I have heard it said that God speaks to us twenty-four hours a day, seven days a week. If we believe that God is with us and guiding us, why is it so hard to believe that he is always talking to us? The reason we have such trouble listening to God is that there are a multitude of distractions we allow to get in the way.

Sometimes, however, God will shove his way through the distractions to give us a message he wants us to hear. Listening to God in this way is the gift of revelation. They are messages God gives us for our benefit and the benefit of others.

One of the ways God can speak to us is through a private revelation. I experienced this once when I was praying about changing jobs. I had a job that was very difficult for me, and there was no peace in my heart. I applied at several places hoping to get a better job, but there was one job that seemed custom-made for me. The interview went great, and I believed it was the answer to my prayer.

A few days later I got a call from the employer telling me they had chosen someone else for the position. I was crushed! Driving to work that morning, I cried out to God, "Don't you care that I'm miserable in this job?!" And then I sensed his voice asking me in the depths of my heart, "Do you love me more than you hate your job?"

As soon as I could admit that I did love God more than I hated my job, an incredible peace came over me. It was a peace that carried me through the remaining time I worked there. What I later discovered was that had I resigned, it would have been one of the worst decisions I ever made.[71] God knows what he's doing. So, God can give us a personal message in prayer or whenever he wants to.

Another way God can speak to us is as a group or community member. A friend of mine sensed God speak to him at the beginning of the Coronavirus pandemic. In the prophecy God said,

> Hear Me, My people! Hear the cry of My voice! For I am with you! I am within you, and I am upholding you! Do not fear the threat that you see around you! Did I not deliver Daniel in the lion's den? Did I not deliver Shadrach, Meshach, and Abednego in the fiery furnace? As I delivered them in, and I repeat in their afflictions, so I will deliver you in yours!

The purpose of prophecy is to give encouragement and exhortation to a group. Another form of prophecy is directed more toward an individual than a group. It's called word of knowledge.

---

71   I was teaching a secondary special education class and was having a difficult time with it. Had I resigned I might not have ever been hired anywhere again.

My wife Kathy and I were at a charismatic prayer meeting one night when she received a message from the Lord. The words started coming to her mentally; her heart began pounding rapidly, and despite her desire not to speak, she knew she had to.

She said, "There is someone here thinking of committing suicide. God does not want you to go through with it. He loves you very much, and if you give him your life, he will bless you." Kathy was initially embarrassed and afraid she had made a mistake.

After the prayer meeting a lady approached her and said, "That was for me." The reason she had come to the prayer meeting that night was a last-ditch effort to find something to give her hope. If she didn't find it at the prayer meeting, she was going to go home and kill herself.

Marcella, a friend of ours, had a similar experience. She was in the waiting room at a local hospital waiting for her daughter to come out of surgery. During her wait, she noticed a lady sitting nearby looking sad. Suddenly, she sensed God's voice: "Go tell her that I love her and that everything's going to be all right."

She hesitated at first, but then she responded to what she sensed God telling her to do. She spoke with the lady and discovered that she had recently lost her father. Six months before her husband had died, and she was struggling with arthritis.

She had recently told God that if he didn't soon give her a sign of hope, she was going to end it all. But when Marcella gave her God's message she broke down in tears. It was the exact message she needed to hear.

Another time, Marcella was working at a Life in the Spirit Seminar.[72] She suddenly sensed God telling her to speak these words to one of the participants: "God wants you to sing again." Marcella had no idea who this lady was.

After Marcella gave her this message, the lady told her that at one time she was constantly singing. In fact, they had called her, "the Singer" at work. But after her husband died, she sank into such a deep depression that she hadn't sung a note. God was telling her she needed to start singing again. How wonderful that God knows exactly what we need when we need it.

A Catholic charismatic prayer meeting is an ideal place to learn about and practice using the gift of prophecy.[73] By using the word "practice," I'm not saying that everyone has this gift, and we need to practice using it. But the best place to learn about this gift and how to use it is at a Catholic charismatic prayer meeting.

---

72 This is a seminar for people wanting to receive the baptism in the Holy Spirit.
73 The view that no one has all the gifts is pretty well stated by St. Paul in Romans 12:3–8, 1 Corinthians 12:4–10 and 12–31.

Now, while we may not all have the gift of prophecy, we all have a prophetic gifting through the sacrament of baptism. At our baptism, we became priest, prophet, and king. Our prophetic calling is to let others know the mystery of the universe![74]

Our prophetic calling is to let others know that God is real, loves them, and has a wonderful plan for their lives. We also have an insight into future events. Evil is going to increase (CCC 675), but in the end, evil will be conquered by Jesus Christ! (Revelation 20:10) Indeed, evil has already been conquered by Jesus Christ through his death on the cross (CCC 672). Our prophetic mission is to invite those who do not know Jesus to be on the winning team!

So, through our baptism we already have a prophetic ministry, although we may not all have the gift of prophecy. But we are all called to share the good news of Jesus Christ.

What is important is being obedient to God. If we sense God speaking prophetically to us, we need to speak his word out. If it is not of God, he will let us know. It may result in a momentary embarrassment but are we willing to be embarrassed for Jesus? On the other hand, it could also be God wanting to deliver a message through us.

God can also give someone a mental image of a message. Mental images are different from the visons mentioned by

---

74 See Ephesians 1:7–10.

St. Teresa of Avila[75] and St. John of the Cross.[76] Mystical visions are meant specifically for the one receiving them. Mental images, on the other hand, are akin to the gift of prophecy. It is a message the Lord has for the community.[77]

One night at our prayer meeting, Patricia (one of our members) said the Lord had given her a mental image of a huge bonfire. From the bonfire, flames were being shot-out in different directions. The message she received from this image of the bonfire was symbolic of our praises to God. As we continued praising God, the bonfire grew bigger with embers being sent all over the city.

One ember might be sent to someone in prison needing to be touched by God. Another ember might be sent to someone in depression needing a touch of hope. Another ember might be sent to someone struggling with a temptation to sin. The message to our community was that our praises went beyond our own edification. God was ministering far beyond our walls through them.

---

[75] St. Teresa of Avila, *The Interior Castle, Book VI*, trans. Kieran Kavanaugh and Otilio Rodriguez. Washington, D.C. ICS Publications. 1980. Chapters 8 and 9.

[76] St. John of the Cross, *The Ascent to Mount Carmel, Book 2* trans. Kieran Kavanaugh and Otilio Rodriguez. Washington, D.C. ICS Publications. chapters 16 and 23.

[77] St. John of the Cross, *The Ascent to Mount Carmel, Book 3* chapter 30, #2.

In 1 Corinthians 14:1, St. Paul tells us to "strive eagerly for the spiritual gifts, above all that you may prophesy" (NAB). As I mentioned before, one of the best places to learn how to use the various forms of prophecy is at a Catholic charismatic prayer meeting. Once we understand how prophecy works, we can take this gift into the marketplace. After all, God's intention for the gifts of the Holy Spirit is to continue Jesus's ministry in the world.

Discernment of Spirits

One more gift I want to mention is the discernment of spirits. In 1 Peter 5:8, we're told, "Be sober and vigilant. Your opponent the devil is prowling around like a roaring lion looking for someone to devour." This text will come up again in the chapter on spiritual warfare.

As was mentioned earlier in chapter 5, the discernment of spirits is a sense that something isn't right. Whether it's with a person, a situation, or a decision being made, there is the awareness that something isn't right. There might even be a sense of evil being present.

One day my wife and I entered a bookstore, and she suddenly became aware of the presence of evil. Then she saw a sign directing people to a room to have their fortunes told. That is what was causing her to sense the presence of evil. The Church firmly states that we are not to have anything to do with fortunetelling or anything claiming to have knowledge of future events (CCC 2116–2117). This will be discussed more in chapter 10.

Kathy's peace began to decrease even more when she saw a lady enter the room. A sense of urgency came over her, and she would not leave the store until she spoke with the lady. Once the lady left the room, Kathy approached her and said, "You don't need to go to a fortune teller. God loves you very much, and if you give your life to him, he'll take care of you." The lady thanked her and walked off.

The conversation didn't go any further, but a seed was planted. What is important is that Kathy did what she sensed she had to do because of the evil she was sensing in her spirit. Some people might not go as far as Kathy did, but they will at least know to pray for that person or situation.

Another example of discernment of spirits occurred at a business where a friend had applied for a job. He was later offered the job but declined to accept it because he could sense something evil in the establishment. He later found out it was run by Satanists. The discernment of spirits can also help us deal with people in everyday situations.

But discernment can also enlighten us about something good. When I was in formation for the diaconate, we occasionally were told, "You're not deacons yet!" The insinuation being that we could be asked to leave formation at a moment's notice.

I think some of the men were intimidated by this, but I knew in my heart it was God's will for me to be a deacon. I sometimes felt like saying, "If God wants me to be a deacon, there's nothing you're going to do about it!" Of course, had I actually said that I might have discovered differently.[78]

---

78 "Jesus answered him, "Again it is written, 'You shall not put the Lord, your God, to the test" (Matthew 4:7.)

Questions for Thought and Discussion

Discovering the Gifts of Revelation

1. Briefly describe a time that God has spoken to you. What was the message? How did you respond to it?

2. Describe a situation when you wanted to hear God's voice but were unable to. In what ways were you seeking to hear his voice??

3. Although God may speak to us about major situations, can we also expect him to speak to us about trivialities? Why or why not? Give some examples.

4. What do you think is required of us to hear God's voice?

5. How can you discern if a message is from God or not?

6. What will happen if you give a message to someone or a group and it's not of the Lord?

CHAPTER 10
Discovering the Gifts of Service:

Mercy, Hospitality, Giving, Leadership, and Serving in Ministry

Several years ago, a Christian I was working with told me that one of his gifts was the ability to identify gifts in others. That's not one of the gifts mentioned by St. Paul, but I can see how it might be one of the unmentioned gifts of the Holy Spirit. Some people do need to be pushed in the direction God may be calling them in. One of the attributes I admire in some pastors is their ability to discern and call out the gifts they see in members of their flock.

In any case, when I asked him what my gift was, he said, "Mercy." That is not what I wanted to hear. I was hoping he would tell me I had an untapped gift for performing miracles or healing. I apparently wanted a gift that was going to bring me some glory. But personal glory is not the purpose of the gifts of the Holy Spirit, and this is especially true with the "service gifts." Their purpose is to humbly serve behind the scenes.

> The purpose of the gift of serving is to humbly minister behind the scenes.

So, what are these gifts of service? The bible gives several examples of what the service gifts are: serving in ministry (Romans 12:7), giving (Romans 12:8), encouragement (Romans 12:8), leadership (Romans 12:8), mercy (Romans 12:8), hospitality (1 Peter 4:9), and intercessory prayer (Ephesians 6:18). Rather than being separate gifts, though, they are all different parts of the same thing. They are all helping gifts, and many of them work in sync with each other.

Let me introduce you to Nestor and Nellie Baca. They had just returned from a pilgrimage to Medjugorje when they felt a strong calling to give something back to God. They were both successful realtors, made a lot of money, and began to question the need to make more. So, after a year and a half of prayer, they decided to see if there was some way they could serve in Mexico.

Eventually, they got involved with the Lord's Ranch in El Paso, Texas. (This is the community that Fr. Rick Thomas, S.J., was a part of. See page 81) At the Lord's Ranch, Nestor and Nellie started meeting with the prayer group and participating in their various ministries. The prayer group was called *Las Alas* (the Wings). Through this group, they were involved with the prison ministry, prayer at the abortorium, the distribution of food, and other ministries.

One day, as a part of the distribution of food ministry, they met an elderly lady who lived in Juarez. She lived in a ramshackle house made of cardboard and pieces of wood.

Discovering the Gifts of Service

They were deplored by the condition they saw her living in. When they saw that many people in Juarez were living in houses like this, they realized they had to do something about it. So, they got people together and started building houses for them. To this date, they have built at least seventy homes.

They also noticed beggars under a bridge in Juarez who looked very thirsty and hungry. So, they started bringing them bottles of water and passing out bags of lunches. Then when they returned to Albuquerque (they still had a home here) they contacted the Roadrunner food bank and started distributing food once a month from the St. Therese parish gym.

They still minister from time to time in Juarez, and they have been doing this for over twenty years. This is just one example of the gift of service. Those with this gift will tell Jesus, "You have given so much to me, now what can I do for you?" This is true for any of us. If we take the time to focus on our blessings rather than what we do not have, we'll discover that we have been abundantly blessed!

We have all been called to give to a certain degree, but the gifted giver is one who has a special calling for it. The Holy Spirit compels them to give in a variety of ways.

> Jesus, you have given so much to me, now what can I do for you?

This can easily be seen with Nestor and Nellie Baca. Their compassion for the poor in Juarez (mercy) caused them to organize people to help build homes (leadership), requiring them to give and receive donations (giving) and mobilize a system of other helpers. This is evangelization. In doing this they often invited people to stay with them at their home in El Paso (hospitality). This all came from a gift of service.

Those with the gift of service are often doing random acts of kindness. Whenever they see a need, they respond to it. They let people go in front of them in a long line at a store. They pay the difference when a customer is short of cash. They're the first to volunteer, and they rarely complain about the work needing to be done. Their servant antennae are always extended, surveying the ground for a need to be met.

This can clearly be seen in Tim Fresquez. He was brought up in a Catholic family that was committed to their faith. But since his dad owned a bar, drinking alcohol, even to excess, was seen as a normal part of life. So, Tim began drinking at 12 years of age, and at 17 he started using cocaine.

At 23 years of age, Tim was a full-blown alcoholic and drug user. This was his life until he was 40 years old. What changed him was his 90-day prison sentence for DWI. He decided at this time that either his life would change, or he would die. He also stopped seeing this girl who was constantly drawing him back into the alcoholic spiral.

Discovering the Gifts of Service

While in prison, Tim started an Alcoholics Anonymous group for some of the prisoners. He knew how to do this because of the rehabilitation groups he had previously been a part of. Once he left prison, he continued mentoring men for AA and Narcotics Anonymous. When he started seeing a priest, Fr. Javier, for spiritual guidance, he was led to minister in the parish. The first ministry he was a part of was the Passion play.

He has since volunteered as a eucharistic minister, lector, sacristan, homebound minister, and custodian. Whenever there is the need for someone to lead a rosary, perform a graveside service, or help with funerals, Tim is always there to give his support, and he rarely, if ever, complains about it.

It is obvious that Tim has a gift for Service. He received this gift at baptism, but it has grown through his life experience and the power of the Holy Spirit.

> Acts of service for a Christian are visible expressions of Jesus's presence.

Tim always seems to be busy, but he's doing something he loves, and he has it in control. But some with this gift become so active with new projects their former commitments suffer from it. They can burn themselves out. Someone with the gift of service needs to monitor their activities and learn how to *"Just say no!"* But if this gift is in control, it is one of the most important gifts of the Holy Spirit in the Church today.

When someone sees a member of the Church doing random acts of kindness, they begin to wonder what it is about that person that makes them so different. This sense of wonder will also minister to those outside the Church. Their questioning will enable them to hear God's voice more clearly when he speaks to them through their conscience.

The gift of service is a powerful source of evangelization, especially in a secular-oriented world. People hear televangelists boast about the love of God and how faith in Jesus can change their lives. But when they see members of the Church acting no differently than they do, it's a hard argument to sell. But what the Christian servant shows the secular world is that there is a difference.

Intercessory Prayer

Intercessory prayer is a gift that is not included in any of St. Paul's lists but should be. We often see prayer as an individual communing with God. Through meditation, perseverance, and silence, we are drawn into a more intimate relationship with God. This is all true.

But when we pray for others, our intercession becomes an indispensable act of service. Its importance lies in the fact that many ministries and individuals are surviving only by someone's prayerful support.

A leader, for instance, can call a group to action, but it is the Holy Spirit who will ignite the fire within them. This comes from prayer. People might think that serving in a particular way is a good idea, but it is the Holy Spirit who is going to motivate them to act. This comes from prayer. Someone might be extremely limited in their resources, but prayer will enable them to feed the multitudes.

One of the problems with the Church today is there are not enough intercessors. In Isaiah 59:16, God looked upon the earth and was appalled that he couldn't find a single intercessor. The situation in our Church might not be the same today, but are there enough intercessors? Could God be calling you to be an intercessor?

An intercessor is one who hungers and thirsts to pray for the needs of others because they know God answers prayer. If this desire to pray for others is not already in our hearts, we can ask God to grant it to us. If we can see the need for this gift, then it is a sign we may already have it. The next step is to start praying.

Intercessory prayer can also be done by offering God our suffering and sacrifices. In Colossians 1:24, St. Paul tells us, "Now I rejoice in my sufferings for your sake, and in my flesh, I am filling up what is lacking in the afflictions of Christ on behalf of his body, which is the church" (NAB). What this means is that we each have the opportunity to share in the salvation of the world by uniting our suffering with that of Jesus Christ.[79]

---

[79] This point is confirmed by Pope John Paul II, in the apostolic letter, "Salvifici Doloris: On the Christian Meaning of Human Suffering," (February 11, 1984), #19 Vatican website.

When we unite our sufferings with Jesus's for others, we contribute to their spiritual benefit and the alleviation of their suffering. This is true whether the healing is physical, psychological, financial, relational, or what have you. I believe Jesus is going to be more apt to answer a request made through suffering because it is a request made with great love and sacrifice.

A few years ago, for instance, I had a bad case of double pneumonia. I was constantly coughing, had trouble sleeping, and it was hard for me to breathe. So, I offered it up for a friend who had a rare form of cancer. He is completely healed from cancer at this time. I know that several other people were praying for him, but I am confident that in some way, God did answer my prayer. Furthermore, it gave meaning to the suffering I was going through.

Another example of someone offering their suffering for others was St. Maria Faustina Kowalska (1905–1938). Jesus had revealed to her that her suffering would benefit others (Diary of Saint Maria Faustina Kowalska #67). On one occasion, there was a young lady who was being tempted to commit suicide. Sr. Kowalska was praying for this student when suddenly the saint became quite ill.

Faustina suffered tremendously for a week, and then suddenly, the suffering was gone. It ended at the exact time the student was freed from the desire to kill herself. St. Faustina attributed the student's emotional healing to the offering of her suffering (Diary of Saint Maria Faustina Kowalska #192).

As we share in Christ's suffering for others, we will discover that "suffering is present in the world in order to release love, in order to give birth to works of love toward neighbor, [and] in order to transform the whole of human civilization into a 'civilization of love.'" [80]

Offering our suffering for others and all the gifts of service are about doing acts of love for Jesus.[81]

---

80 John Paul 11, *Salvifici Doloris*. 1984. Vatican Website. February 11, 1984. #30.
81 "Amen, I say to you, whatever you did for one of these least brothers of mine, you did for me" (Matthew 25:40).

Questions for Thought and Discussion

Discovering the Gifts of Service

1. Do you know someone with the gifts of service? What are some of the attributes you admire and would like to have?

2. In John 13:14 Jesus tells us to wash one another's feet. Give some examples of how this can be done in the real world.

3. In Colossians 1:24 St. Paul says, "Now I rejoice in my sufferings for your sake." How do you think St. Paul, Pope John Paul 11, and St. Faustina found joy in their suffering? Give some examples of how we can find joy in our suffering.

4. The idea of tithing 10 percent of our income to God comes from the word "tithe," which means one-tenth. What are some other ways we can tithe to the Church?

5. In the story of the "Widows Mite," (Mark 12:41–44, Luke 21:1–4) Jesus told his disciples that the few pennies the widow put into the treasury were greater than the wealth others had contributed. Why is this a good scripture for talking about the gift of service?

"I can do all things through Christ who Strengthens me."

Philippians 4:13- KJV

CHAPTER 11
Discovering the Ephesians 4:11 Gifts:

Apostleship, Evangelization, and Pastoring

The gifts mentioned in Ephesians 4:11 are apostles, prophets, evangelists, and pastors. Since I have already dealt with the gift of prophecy and teaching, I'll leave these alone. We'll begin, then, with the gift of apostleship. Many people don't think of apostleship as being a gift because they associate it with the twelve apostles. We're not ever going to be one of them. What, then, is the gift of apostleship?

Apostleship is the first gift St. Paul mentions in 1 Corinthians 12:28. The word itself means, "One who is sent." At face value, this can pertain to all followers of Jesus Christ. As I have mentioned elsewhere in the book, we are all called to bring Jesus's presence to those we meet.

The one with the gift of apostleship is called to "get things started." They recognize a need that isn't being met, and they meet that need. An example is someone who begins a missionary activity or plants a church. The idea is they get something new started, form leaders, and then move on. This was typical of what the twelve apostles did, including and especially St. Paul.

But I believe the gift of apostleship can also belong to those who see a need, develop a ministry to meet that need, and stay with it for a while. My development of the LIGHT Seminar is an example of this. Its purpose is to acquaint on-fire Catholics with the gifts of the Holy Spirit and their use in everyday life. In my interaction with different Catholic groups, it seemed like there was a need for this type of ministry.

Another example of apostleship is a program for Catholics who are divorced. A few years ago, Jane Zingelman, a Catholic divorcee, couldn't find anything in her area for divorced Catholics. One day she heard Rose Sweet interviewed on the local Catholic radio station. She spoke about a thirteen-week video program that she had developed called *Surviving Divorce*.

When Jane heard Rose speak about her program, the Holy Spirit quickened in her heart, and she knew this was something that needed to be developed locally. She purchased the video and went through the program herself. Afterward, Jane contacted several parishes to see if any were interested. Eventually, a parish gave her their blessing, and she began the *Divorce Recovery Ministry*.

They met once a week to view the thirteen videos offered by *Surviving Divorce*, followed by discussion and prayer. This spun off into two related ministries. The first spin-off was a book club. They each got a book that Jane recommended, read it, and discussed the contents. These were books dealing with relationships, marriage, divorce, spirituality, etc.

Another spin-off was a "meet-up" that was held once a month after Mass. Each participant got an article on a subject similar to those in the book club. They read the article together and discussed it. All of this came from Jane recognizing a need in the Church and finding a way to meet that need.

The question we need to ask ourselves is, do I see a need in the Church and a way to meet that need? Do I have a gift of apostleship that I'm not using? We're not all called to this, but we need to ask God for the grace to respond if this is his will for us.

Another gift from Ephesians 4:11 is "evangelization." The gift of evangelization is the hunger in a believer's heart to share the Good News with others. There is a certain level where every Catholic/Christian is commanded to be an evangelist.

In Matthew 28:19 Jesus says, "Go, therefore, and make disciples of all nations, baptizing them in the name of the Father, and of the Son, and of the Holy Spirit, teaching them to observe all that I have commanded you" (NAB). Although this command is often seen as pertaining to the clergy, the Church recognizes that all followers of Jesus have a role to play in evangelization (CCC 905–907).

The call to evangelize is further given in 1 Peter 3:15 where we're told, "Always be ready to give an explanation to anyone who asks you for a reason for your hope but do it with gentleness and reverence" (NAB.)

This is speaking to all followers of Jesus Christ. This doesn't mean that we all have to be witnessing door to door, passing out tracts in the mall or preaching on the street corner. There is a place for this but not everyone is called to it. Even though we are called to share our faith with others, there are those who have a special gift for this.

One of these was a friend of mine named John Fidel. John has gone home to be with the Lord, but in the years that I knew him he was a textbook example of someone with the gift of evangelization. Frequently, we would have breakfast or lunch together at a restaurant. We would often be sharing something about Jesus, the Church, and the gifts of the Holy Spirit.

On several occasions, people came over to our table with questions, wanting to know more about our faith in Jesus Christ. Immediately, John would start witnessing to them with gentleness and respect. Often, he would end up praying with them. One time we were standing in line at a cafeteria. While I was deciding whether to have fish or Salisbury steak, I glanced over at John and saw that he was telling the lady next to him about Jesus Christ.

Another time John was working out in the gym when he saw a lady looking rather despondent leaning against a pillar. Her name was Betty Braswell. John approached her and said, "Do you think you can push over that pillar?" Betty told him she was sure the pillar would hold her and her frustrations up very well. John asked, "What frustrations? Let's take a walk." John and Betty had never met each other before.

As they walked around the interior of the gym, John asked Betty if she knew that Jesus lived in her heart. Since this is what she had been taught in her Catholic faith, she told John, of course she knew this. But when John explained that she could experience Jesus's presence and his love for her, she said, "This is what I want. How do I get it?"

John told her that Jesus was in her heart already. She just needed to ask Jesus to come to life within her. He prayed with her in the middle of the gym, she received Jesus in her heart and was filled with incredible joy. The awareness of God's presence and his love has not left her since.

So, while God had blessed John with the gift of evangelization, he had been the beneficiary of someone else having this gift. At this time, John was not the evangelical powerhouse he had become. He was the manager of a bar in a hotel restaurant where his foul language had become a common occurrence. One day a lady approached him holding a paperback book in her hand. She said, "You have a filthy mouth, and you need to read this book!" She handed him the copy of the book she was carrying.

The name of the book was, *Nine O'clock in the Morning*, by Dennis Bennett. This is the true account of an Episcopalian priest who received baptism in the Holy Spirit and began sharing this experience with others. This was the beginning of the ecumenical, charismatic renewal.

John was a nominal Catholic and wasn't too concerned about this woman's opinion of him. But he took the book home and began to read it. He said that he read the entire book, and very early in the morning, sitting in the kitchen in his underwear, he gave his life to Jesus Christ. If it hadn't been for this woman's desire to share her faith, her gift of evangelization, John would not have shared his faith with Betty or the many other people he was able to minister to.

Now, we won't all have a gift for evangelization at the level that John Fidel did, but we are still called to share our faith with others. And since God has called us to this, he has also given us a certain level of this gift that he expects us to use. If we ask God to make us aware of these evangelical moments, he will do it. If we ask God for the courage to respond to these moments, he will do that as well. The only thing left for us is to evangelize.

The last gift I want to mention from Ephesians 4:11 is that of pastoring. It's logical to assume that this gift will be given to pastors and Church leaders. Nonetheless, this gift can also be given to parents.

In the Decree on the Apostolate of Lay People from the Documents of Vatican II [82] we're told that the family is the "domestic sanctuary of the Church." Parents are responsible for bringing their children up in the faith. Often this is left to clergy and teachers of religion. The Church reminds parents that "They are the first to pass on the faith to their children and to educate them in it."[83]

Parents can pray with their children, read bible stories, and model Jesus's love. They can take them to Mass, discuss religious topics, and encourage the children to grow in their faith. Parents are in a primary position to model and teach their children about having a relationship with God.

Children want to be like their parents. If they see that a relationship with God is important to their parents, it will be important for them too. The children might eventually turn from the faith, but they will still have the spiritual foundation their parents provided. When they are ready to have a relationship with Jesus themselves, they will already have a foundation to build on.

When I was growing up, it was my mom who responded to this gift of pastoring. She prayed with me at bedtime, made sure we always prayed before meals, took us to Mass regularly, and sent me to Catholic school from the first through the eighth grades. Since my dad wasn't very religious, it was my

---

[82] Vatican II, *The Decree on the Apostolate of Lay People* (November 18, 1965) #11, Vatican website.
[83] Vatican II, #11.

mom who ensured our faith was provided for. My dad never opposed her in this, but he would not have provided for us spiritually himself.

Just prior to my eighth-grade year, my parents were divorced, and the man my mom married was a nonpracticing Methodist. He saw no reason for practicing his own faith, let alone becoming Catholic.

My mom was no longer practicing her faith, nor was I. About six years later I met Jesus through the Catholic Charismatic Renewal, and everything I learned from my mom's spiritual pastoring came back to me. It all began to make sense now.

For a while, it might have seemed like all my mom's efforts had gone down the tubes. But the spiritual foundation she formed in me drew me back to Jesus. This is what a domestic pastor does.

Any leader in the Church can use the gift of pastoring. The way we do this is by becoming an ambassador for Jesus Christ[84] to the flock we are called to serve. The image of a pastor is a shepherd taking care of his or her flock, and the ultimate shepherd is Jesus Christ. He is the shepherd of all shepherds.

---

84 "So, we are ambassadors for Christ, as if God were appealing through us. We implore you on behalf of Christ, be reconciled to God" (2 Corinthians 5:20).

Questions for Thought and Discussion

Discovering the Ephesians 4:11 Gifts: Apostleship, Evangelization, and Pastoring

1. Name someone you know with the gift of apostleship? What did they start? In what way did this meet a certain need?

2. If you could start something in the Church today what would it be?

3. How would you define evangelization? Name someone you believe has the gift of evangelization.

4. What do you think some of the characteristics are of someone with this gift?

5. What are some different ways that someone can evangelize?

6. What are some characteristics of a pastor?

7. Do you think a strong leader will always be a good pastor? Why or why not?

8. Can you think of other positions or situations that someone could have the gift of pastoring?

9. How could the recognition of the Ephesians 4:11 gifts help someone grow in their gift?

*Praise the Lord all you nations! Extol him
All you peoples! His mercy for us is strong;
The faithfulness of the Lord is forever.
Hallelujah!*

-Psalm 117 NAB

CHAPTER 12

Overcoming Obstacles to Living the Spirit-filled Life

Many people have gifts of the Holy Spirit without being aware of it. We've briefly discussed what some of these gifts are and how they can be used in everyday life. Even with this knowledge, though, there are obstacles that need to be overcome for these gifts to come to life within us.

The first obstacle is the belief that God doesn't love us. This might come from a feeling of unworthiness, an awareness of our sins, or doubting that God is powerful enough to personally love everyone in the world. Or someone might believe that God loves them as a member of the human race, but not personally.

This is a problem because if I don't believe God loves me personally, then I'm not going to believe he has personally given me gifts of the Holy Spirit. This is one of Satan's most deceiving weapons in keeping Christians from receiving the abundant life. It is the belief that God is not powerful enough or loving enough to personally care for us.

Overcoming Obstacles to Living the Spirit-filled Life

This is a temptation I was faced with when I was first prayed with to receive the baptism in the Holy Spirit. Expecting to receive the same joy that I had heard others speak about, I didn't receive anything. The person praying with me said, "Don't worry. God works with each of us in different ways." But the first thought that came to me was how unworthy I was to receive this gift. Who was I to think God was going to grant me this experience of his love? Who was I to receive the gifts of the Holy Spirit? I shared about this in chapter 2.

Sometimes trials will give the devil an opportunity to attack us with doubts about God's love. A Roman Catholic priest named Monsignor [85] Scott Friend was diagnosed several years ago with multiple sclerosis. This is a very debilitating disease. It affects the nerves in the brain and the spinal cord resulting in pain, weakness, vision loss, lack of coordination, and fatigue. The duration and severity of this disease can vary from one person to the next, but ultimately there is no current cure for it.

When Fr. Friend first discovered he had this disease, he became very angry with God. Here he had given his life to God as a priest, and this is how he was being repaid? But as he began to praise God despite the disease, he became filled with an incredible awareness of God's peace and love.

---

85 "Monsignor" is an honorific title given to some priests and one that Fr. Friend has. For brevity's sake I'm going to refer to him simply as Fr. Friend. He gave me permission to use his story.

Today he rejoices in the gift of having multiple sclerosis because he believes that without it, he would not have had the level of awareness of God's love that he has since experienced. He also sees this gift as an opportunity to share in the sufferings of Christ. [86]

One of the ways we can deal with these doubts is by inserting our name in the promises God has made to us in scripture. For instance, we can reflect on John 3:16 [87] with a slight change in the wording. Instead of saying, "For God so loved *the world* that he gave his only begotten Son," say, "For God so loved [your name] that he gave his only begotten Son." You can also say, "For God so loved *me* that he gave his only begotten Son."

Another good scripture is Jeremiah 29:11–12: "For I know well the plans I have in mind for you [your name], plans for your welfare and not for woe, so as to give you a future of hope" (NAB). If I used Isaiah 43:1–4 for myself, it would read: "But now, *Michael,* thus says the Lord, who created you, and formed you. Do not fear, for I have redeemed you… you are precious in my sight, *Michael.* You are honored and I love you" (adapted from NAB).

---

86 A video of Msgr. Friend can be seen on YouTube at *What My Faith Means to Me-Msgr. Scott Friend*

87 "For God so loved the world that he gave his only Son, so that everyone who believes in him might not perish but might have eternal life" (NAB).

The idea is to take a promise of God and read it as addressed to you personally. Jesus used Scripture when Satan tempted him, and we should too.

There are also times when God will speak to us through someone else. Shortly after my conversion, I struggled with deep-seated feelings of inferiority. (Heck, to a certain degree, I still struggle with them.) But when I was nineteen to twenty years old, I was really having a struggle with it. I didn't feel like I was worthy to receive any of the gifts of the Holy Spirit or to be used by God.

One night at a prayer meeting, a lady had a prophecy that I felt was meant specifically for me. She said, "How dare you say that you're not worthy! I sent my Son to die for you to make you worthy! How dare you say that you're not worthy!" That prophecy has stuck with me all my life. While it is true that none of us are worthy of God's love, it is through Jesus Christ that we have been made worthy.

Another area that can affect our spirituality is dabbling in the occult. The occult is anything that claims to have supernatural power apart from God. Examples are astrology, fortune telling, tarot cards, Ouija board, horoscopes, witchcraft, Reiki (or supernatural healing apart from God), channeling, and so on.

Many people, and even some Christians, claim there's nothing wrong with these. They're either seen as being innocent forms of amusement or something completely separate from our relationship with God. Some people are just fascinated by their mystique. The Catholic Church, however, completely condemns the occult.

In the Catechism of the Catholic Church #2116 we read:

All forms of divination are to be rejected: recourse to Satan or demons, conjuring up the dead or other practices falsely supposed to "unveil" the future, consulting horoscopes, astrology, palm reading, interpretation of omens and lots, the phenomena of clairvoyance, and recourse to mediums all conceal a desire for power over time, history, and, in the last analysis, other human beings, as well as a wish to conciliate hidden powers. They contradict the honor, respect, and loving fear that we owe God alone.

Not only are occult practices condemned by the Church because they are false but participating in them can open someone up to demonic influences. In other words, it's saying yes to the devil and giving him some control of our lives.

For instance, trusting in the stars to guide us through life is saying that we don't trust God in charge of our lives. The devil's job is to get us to place our trust in something besides God. Some people might initially look at their horoscope out of interest, but they often find that they expect or hope for the predictions to take place.

It might begin as a simple curiosity, but it can develop into a habit and a belief system. Growing in our faith in God isn't easy, and it becomes even more of a struggle when a distractor is thrown in to cloud our faith. This is the devil's goal with any form of the occult.

In CCC 2117 we're told:

All practices of magic or sorcery, by which one attempts to tame occult powers so as to place them at one's service and have a supernatural power over others—even if this were for the sake of restoring their health—are gravely contrary to the virtue of religion. These practices are to be even more condemned when accompanied by the intention of harming someone or when they have recourse to the intervention of demons. Wearing charms is also reprehensible. *Spiritism* often implies divination or magical practices; the Church, for her part, warns the faithful against it. Recourse to so-called traditional cures does not justify either the invocation of evil powers or the exploitation of another's credulity.

So, what does this all mean? If we want to live a Spirit-filled life, grow in our relationship with God, and stay out of the clutches of the evil one, we absolutely have to stay out of the occult. If we have been involved with the occult, we need to renounce it in Jesus's name and stay away from it.

One of the ways we can renounce the occult is by reciting our baptismal promises. It never hurts to remind ourselves and the spiritual world of the promises we have made.

Baptismal Promises[88]

Leader: Do you reject Satan?

Response: I do

Leader: And all his works?

Response: I do.

Leader: And all his empty promises?

Response: I do.

Leader: Do you believe in God, the Father Almighty, creator of heaven and earth?

Response: I do.

Leader: Do you believe in Jesus Christ, his only Son, our Lord, who was born of the Virgin Mary, was crucified,

---

[88] The baptismal promises are taken from the *Rite of Christian Initiation of Adults* New York: Catholic Book Publishing CO. 1988, 157, #C.

died, and was buried, rose from the dead, and is now seated at the right hand of the Father?

Response: I do.

Leader: Do you believe in the Holy Spirit, the holy Catholic Church, the communion of saints, the resurrection of the body, and life everlasting?

Response: I do.

Leader: God, the all-powerful Father of our Lord Jesus Christ, has given us a new birth by water and the Holy Spirit and forgiven all our sins. May he also keep us faithful to our Lord, Jesus Christ forever and ever. Amen.

Another area we need to cover is clinging to unforgiveness. Jesus tells us, in Matthew 6:14:

> If you forgive others their transgressions, your heavenly Father will forgive you. But if you do not forgive others, neither will your Father forgive your transgressions (NAB).

There is a similar text in Mark 11:25:

> When you stand to pray, forgive anyone against whom you have a grievance so that your heavenly Father may in turn forgive you your transgressions (NAB).

Forgiveness, or at least the willingness to forgive, is a VERY BIG DEAL with God! In

> God takes forgiveness very seriously!

Matthew 18:21–35, Jesus tells the story about a servant who owed his master a great deal of money. Some translations have this at 10,000 talents of gold or millions of dollars. When his master threatened to sell him and his family to repay the debt, the servant pleaded for mercy. Having mercy on his servant, the master forgave the entire debt.

The servant later came across another servant owing him a hundred denarii or a few dollars. The servant pleaded with his fellow servant for mercy, but he was given none. Instead, he was put into prison until he paid the entire debt.

On hearing what had happened, the master recanted his forgiveness from the first servant and had him put into prison. Jesus finished the story saying, "So will my heavenly Father do to you, unless each of you forgives his brother from his heart" (NAB).

Jesus has forgiven us all our sins through his death on the cross. It is his free gift to those who will receive it.[89] There is nothing we have done to earn this salvation.[90] But there is the expectation on the part of Jesus Christ that we will forgive others as he has forgiven us.

---

89 "The wages of sin is death, but the gift of God is eternal life in Christ Jesus our Lord" (Romans 6:23).
90 "For by grace you have been saved through faith, and this is not from you, so no one may boast" (Ephesians 2:8–9).

We give God permission to do this when we pray the Our Father: "Forgive us our trespasses as we forgive those who trespass against us." This prayer should give us pause to consider those we have not yet forgiven because our forgiveness is dependent on it.

It is understandable that someone may have been hurt so deeply that it seems impossible for them to forgive. But, what Jesus requires of us is to at least have the desire to forgive. God can work with that. What God can't work with is someone who has decided they will never forgive the one who has wronged them. Not only will this decision keep them from growing spiritually, but it will also hurt them physically and psychologically.

Questions for Thought and Discussion

Overcoming Obstacles for Living a Spirit-Filled Life

1. Can you think of other obstacles for growing in the Spirit-filled life? What are they? What can be done to alleviate them?

2. Why do you think it's hard for some people to believe God loves them personally?

3. What can you do to make others aware of God's love for them?

4. What are some things you can do to be more aware of God's love?

5. Why do you think so many people are drawn to the occult these days?

6. Do you think that popular fiction glorifying the occult can be used to teach Christian values? Why or why not? If you believe it can, how would you do this?

7. Why is the recitation of our baptismal promises a good step to take when renouncing the occult?

8. Why do you think forgiveness is so important to God?

9. How can you forgive someone when you still feel hurt by them? What steps can be taken?

*"If you forgive others their transgressions,
Your heavenly Father will forgive you.
But if you do not forgive others, neither will
Your Father forgive your transgressions."*

-Matthew 6:14-16- NAB

CHAPTER 13
The Prayer of Forgiveness

Occasionally it's good to reflect on some instances where there might be a need for forgiveness in our lives. For this reason, we have a prayer of forgiveness to assist with the reflection process. Read each text in the reflection slowly, pausing at the end of each line, giving time to listen to the Holy Spirit.

Not every line of text will address an area needing your forgiveness. If you do come to an area where you recognize the need for forgiveness, stay there with the Lord. Call to mind the person and the instance needing to be forgiven and then say, "I forgive **[name]** for **[name what they did that needs your forgiveness]** in Jesus's name. If you can't forgive them, then ask for the grace to forgive them. Remember that forgiveness is a choice. You can choose to forgive someone whether you feel like it or not.

Opening Prayer

God, it is my desire to be completely set free from any unforgiveness that I might have in the depths of my heart. Please remind me of any unforgiveness that I might not be aware of and grant me the freedom to forgive those that need to be forgiven.

Forgiving God

Lord, I forgive you for those times you appeared to be absent in my life.

I especially want to forgive you for allowing my loved one(s) to die when I prayed for their healing.

I forgive you for the emptiness their passing made me feel. Help me to know that death is the ultimate healing and that you did answer my prayer.

I forgive you for the poor start I had in life. I was not born in a family of wealth or with many of the advantages that others do.

I forgive you for not granting me these advantages

I forgive you that I am not as talented or as attractive as I would like to be.

I forgive you for not giving me the opportunities that others have had.

Lord, I forgive you for all my disappointments in life and for anything else that has caused me to be angry with you.

You are not to blame for any of these, but I have held you responsible for them in my heart.

Grant me the grace to let the anger go and to be filled with the joy of your forgiveness.

Forgiving Myself

Lord, with your grace, I forgive myself for not taking advantage of the educational and life opportunities that have come to me.

I forgive myself for hurting others, whether intentional or not, and I pray they would receive the grace to forgive me.

I forgive myself for not being a better son, daughter, sister, brother, or friend. I could kick myself for some of the things I said and did.

There were also some things I should have said or done but did not.

I forgive myself for the life choices that didn't turn out so well for me.

Lord, it is especially difficult for me to forgive myself for the times I deliberately turned from you and your love for me. For those times, I ask for your forgiveness and for the grace to forgive myself.

The Prayer of Forgiveness

Forgiving Parents

Lord, I want to thank you for my parents. We didn't always see eye to eye, but I want to thank you for them anyway. I know they did the best they could, even though it didn't seem that way at the time. So, I want to take this opportunity to forgive them.

I forgive them for the times they didn't even try to understand me or the things I was going through. That's how it seemed to me, at least.

I forgive them for the times I was beaten or punished, whether I deserved it or not.

I forgive them for the times they seemed to prefer my brother(s) or sister(s) to me.

I forgive my parents for abandoning me either through divorce, death, being too busy, or pursuing other interests.

I forgive my parents for not encouraging me, taking an interest in my dreams, or showing their love for me.

Forgiving Siblings

Lord, please grant me the grace to forgive my siblings.

It is my desire to forgive the unkind things they said and did to me while we were growing up.

I forgive them for the times they called me names, squealed on me, or stole from me.

I forgive them for the times they abused me or used their strength against me.

I forgive them for getting more ice cream, privileges, or love than I did. This might not have been the way it happened, but it's how I saw it.

I forgive them for not keeping in touch with me.

I forgive them for hurting me physically, emotionally, or spiritually whether they intended to or not.

For any deep-seated hurt that I may not even be aware of now, I forgive them.

Grant them the grace to forgive me for anything I have done to them.

Forgiving Relatives

Lord, I forgive any relatives—uncles, aunts, cousins, nieces, nephews, or grandparents—who have treated me in an unkind or abusive way.

For any unkind words or actions, I forgive them.

I forgive any relative who has hurt my family through lying, cheating, stealing, or taking advantage of our trust.

I forgive them for taking advantage of our generosity.

I forgive them for any inappropriate touching, name-calling, or shaming words they said to me.

I forgive them for exposing me to drugs, alcohol, and/or a lifestyle that made me feel uncomfortable.

Lord, for any way I feel my relatives have hurt me, I forgive them right now.

Forgiving Friends, Acquaintances, and Coworkers

Lord, I pray for the grace to forgive any friends, acquaintances, or coworkers who have hurt me.

I forgive them for the times they stabbed me in the back to improve their position at school, in a group, or with a company.

I forgive them for the times they put me down to give more importance to themselves.

I forgive them for the times they talked behind my back, spread false rumors about me, or tried to ruin my reputation.

I forgive them for bullying me and taking away my peace.

I forgive them for taking something from me because they were jealous of my having it.

I forgive them for any physical or emotional pain they have caused me.

Lord, I thank you for all the good friends, acquaintances, and coworkers I have had. They have been a blessing to me. But it is my desire to forgive each of them who caused pain in my life, or in the lives of those who are dear to me.

If I am having trouble granting any one of them forgiveness for something they either did to me or are doing right now, I pray for the grace to be set free to forgive them from my heart.

I forgive those who have spoken against me or persecuted me in any way for my religious beliefs.

Forgiving Teachers

Lord, God, I thank you for all the good teachers I've had. They have truly been a blessing to me. But I also want to take this opportunity to forgive those teachers who were less than helpful to me.

For those teachers who discouraged me and made me feel like a failure, I forgive them, Lord.

I forgive any teacher for putting me in a low academic group and making me feel stupid.

I forgive those teachers who punished me when I didn't do anything wrong. Sometimes they wouldn't even let me defend myself. I do forgive them, Lord.

I forgive those teachers who were constantly yelling, making school an unpleasant experience.

I forgive those teachers who were boring, silly, or really didn't teach me anything.

I forgive those teachers who made me feel uncomfortable with an inappropriate touch or comment.

I forgive those teachers who punished me in a demeaning way in front of the class.

Lord, I forgive any teacher throughout my earliest to my highest year in school who hurt me in any way at all.

Forgiving Church Leadership

Lord, I forgive any priest, deacon, religious education teacher, youth leader, office staff, pastor, or any person affiliated with the church who has hurt me.

For those responsible for boring homilies and long, drawn-out liturgies, I forgive them, Lord.

For those who belittled or talked down to me whenever I asked a question, I forgive them, Lord.

I forgive any church leader who pressured me into doing something I didn't want to do. They destroyed my faith in the church and in you, my God.

I forgive those church leaders who were too busy to even talk to me.

I forgive those church leaders who were not good models of their faith, causing me to question, or even to lose, my own faith.

I forgive those church leaders who lost their temper and yelled at me over the phone or in person.

I forgive those religious teachers who gave uninspiring and boring classes.

For those representatives of the church who were unkind to others or me personally, I forgive them, Lord.

Please grant me the grace to forgive anyone in the church who has hurt me in any way. It is my desire to forgive them, Lord. Please grant me the grace to forgive them from my heart.

Forgiving Spouses

Lord, I forgive my spouse for the times he/she was impatient with me or wouldn't listen to what I was trying to tell him/her.

I forgive my spouse for trying to punish me with the silent treatment.

I forgive my spouse for not always agreeing with me.

I forgive my spouse for any lack of commitment, showing of love, or giving me encouragement.

I forgive my spouse for leaving me through separation, divorce, or death.

Lord, I forgive my spouse for spending more quality time with others, or their own interests than with me.

I forgive my spouse for wanting to argue more than to listen.

I forgive my spouse for the mean things he/she has said and/or done to me.

I forgive my spouse for being different than when we were first married.

I forgive my spouse for not taking more of an interest in the upkeep of the home and family.

Lord, I forgive my spouse for any anger I have for her/him at this time.

I ask you for the grace to truly forgive [name] from my heart, and I pray [name] would receive the grace to forgive me as well.

Forgiving Others

I forgive any bosses who treated me unfairly, wouldn't give me credit for the good work I did, and only criticized the mistakes I made.

I forgive them for not giving me the promotion I deserved, not giving me a raise, and keeping me from advancing.

I forgive any doctors for their misdiagnosis. I forgive them for not having a good bedside manner.

I forgive those doctors who did not do enough for my loved one(s).

I forgive any lawyer(s), who either did not do a good job of representing me or found ways to hurt me as much as they possibly could.

The Prayer of Forgiveness

I forgive anyone who has sued me.

I forgive anyone who hurt me, resulting in a court case.

I forgive any law enforcement personnel for treating me rougher than I deserved.

I forgive any criminal who has hurt me or those that I love.

I forgive my neighbors for not being as considerate as they should be.

I forgive those drivers who have cut me off in traffic, made obscene gestures, or ran me off the road. I forgive that driver who ran into my car, causing an accident.

I forgive the drunk or reckless driver who caused the death of my loved one(s).

I forgive the computer tech who sent the virus that crashed my computer.

I forgive the person who stole my identity, withdrawing money from my bank account.

Summary Prayer

Lord, I choose right now to forgive anyone I have yet to forgive. And if I am not able to forgive them right now,

I pray for the grace to be able to forgive them in the near future. If I have no desire to forgive them, I ask you for the grace to have this desire. It is my desire to serve you, God, and if my unforgiveness is going to keep me from this, then I want to be able to forgive. I pray this in Jesus's name. Amen.

CHAPTER 14

Discovering Daily Growth

Some people think that when they've received their sacraments, been prayed-with to receive the release of the Holy Spirit or surrendered their lives to Jesus Christ, there's nothing more out there. They think there's nothing more they have to give to God, or that God has to give to them. The next step is heaven, or purgatory, or whatever the afterlife holds.

The truth is that this is only the beginning of what God has prepared for us! What God wants us to do for him after we've received these blessings is to make our hearts docile to the Holy Spirit. He wants us to give him free rein to work in us and through us.

I like to compare this to uniting ourselves with Jesus on the cross. St. Paul tells us in Romans 6:6, "We know that our old self was crucified with him, so that our sinful body might be done away with, that we might no longer be in slavery to sin" (NAB). As Jesus's body was crucified and put to death on the cross, so must our sinful habits be crucified and put to death. Rest assured I am not talking about making ourselves holy. Only God can do that. But we can cooperate with God's grace in becoming the people he has created us to be.

So, at the top of the image of a crucifix is Jesus's head, still wearing the crown of thorns. One of the first things we need to be crucified of is our thought life. In the book of Ephesians, we're told:

> Put away the old self of your former way of life, corrupted through deceitful desires, and be renewed in the spirit of your minds, and put on the new self, created in God's way in righteousness and holiness of truth (Eph. 4:22–24, NAB).

At the top of the crucifix with Jesus's head we need to delete the thinking of our former lives and replace it with "the mind of Christ" (1 Corinthians 2:16b). I call this "mental overwrite." We delete our former way of thinking by replacing it with a new way of thinking.

Mental Overwrite

One of the first ways we can do this is to start reading scripture. This should be done on a daily basis. With our busy lifestyles it's best to schedule a daily appointment with God. This schedule may change from time to time, but our appointment with God should be important enough that we won't let it go altogether. And even if we do miss a day or two, this is not the unforgiveable sin. What we want to do is develop a habit of prioritizing the reading of God's Word in our lives.

> The Bible is a love letter from God.

Scripture can be looked at as being God's love letter to each one of us. It is God letting us know who he is, who we are, and how we can live an abundant life. Surely, this is an important bit of information to find out from our creator!

Scripture also helps us to know who Jesus is. After all, "He is the image of the unseen God" (Colossians 1:15, NAB). As we come to know Jesus Christ through reading scripture, we will come to know the God of the universe! The only way we can have a relationship with anyone is by getting to know them. Reading scripture helps us to know who the Father, the Son, and the Holy Spirit are, and what this should mean to us personally.

In reading the New Testament we can also get to know who we are through Jesus Christ. We are adopted children of God.[91] Through Jesus Christ we can call the Father "our Dad!"[92] There is an intimate bond we have with him. The secular world, on the other hand, has given us the image of ourselves as being insignificant. We have to earn being loved by reaching certain standards the culture has created for us.

But God loves us exactly as we are. We have each been created with dignity, worth, and the potential for greatness. As we read scripture and choose to believe what it says, the secular world's view is overwritten and deleted from our memories.

---

91 Ephesians 1:4b–5.
92 Romans 8:15.

This can also take place when we read the spiritual masters of our faith, like St. John of the Cross, St. Teresa of Avila, St. Therese of the Infant Jesus, and other saints. We can get this from reading contemporary spiritual writers. We can get this from reading the daily texts for Mass. The point is to overwrite the false image we have of ourselves and replace it with God's image.

Making Tracks with Our Feet

From the head of Jesus, we move down to his feet nailed to the cross. Jesus once used his feet to move around the countryside, ministering to the needs of others. Our feet often move about in search of meeting their own needs. They ask, "What is it that will give me pleasure, fulfillment, and satisfaction?"

But Jesus's feet moved to wash the feet of others. So, as our feet are nailed to the cross with those of Jesus's, we will begin to die to the constant need for self-preservation. We will begin to recognize the needs of others. We will begin to sense a desire, like St. Mother Teresa of Calcutta, to quench the thirst of Jesus.[93]

But we don't have to wait for this desire to come bubbling forth in our hearts. We can begin serving because Jesus has

---

93 Reference is made to Mother Teresa's thoughts on "quenching the thirst of Jesus" in, *Come Be My Light: The Private Writings of the Saint of Calcutta*, P. 41.

commanded it of us [94] and we want to be obedient to him. Sometimes, we can get a good feeling from serving others, but this shouldn't be our primary motive. We serve because if we love God, we will in fact love others.[95]

This doesn't mean we're necessarily going to feel love for them, or that we're going to feel like serving.

> We need to serve as Jesus served.

But it does mean we have made a commitment to love and a commitment to serve. Jesus didn't go to the cross because he thought it was going to feel good. He did it because he made a choice to love us and be obedient to his Father.

When our feet are nailed to the cross with Jesus's feet, we're going to love and serve for the same reason. The important thing about serving is to keep our intention clear. If we're doing it to ensure a high place in heaven or to make ourselves holy, then we're doing it for the wrong reason.

We serve because we have nailed our feet to Jesus's feet on the cross. In doing so we have made a commitment to continue his work of service. As we choose to serve others, we are quenching the thirst of Jesus Christ.

---

94 Some examples of this can be seen in Matthew 20:26, 25:31–46, Mark 10:43, Luke 10:29–37, and John 15:1–15.
95 "If anyone says, 'I love God,' but hates his brother, he is a liar; for whoever does not love a brother whom he has seen cannot love God whom he has not seen" (1 John 4:20).

The Right Hand of Fellowship

We move now from Jesus's feet on the cross to his right hand nailed through the wrist. This is the hand of community.

> **We need to recognize our need for each other.**

Whenever someone is asked to take an oath, make a pledge, or shake hands with someone it's done with the right hand. There are several places in scripture that mention Jesus sitting at God's right hand as being a special place of honor. So, we can look at Jesus's right hand nailed to the cross as being the hand of fellowship and community.

In community and fellowship, we're telling others they are more important than we are. In Philippians 2:3–4 we're told: "Do nothing from selfishness or conceit, but in humility count others better than yourselves. Let each of you look not only to his own interests, but also to the interests of others" (RSV).

Where our tendency is to put ourselves first, Christian fellowship demands that we put others first. But we don't do it because they need us, and we have something that can benefit them. We do it, rather, because we need them. The ideal community is where the members are aware of their need for each other. This is the idea of community St. Paul gives in Romans 12: 4–8, and 1 Corinthians 12:14–31. We are all members of the body of Christ, and we need each other.

In the Roman Catholic tradition, community has often been seen as attending Mass. This is theologically correct! At Mass, the body of Christ comes together to worship God as "one," to receive Jesus through the Eucharist, and to take Jesus out to the rest of the world. But we are also social beings in need of interacting with each other. We need a medium in which we can share our faith, grow in relationships, and hold each other accountable.

Fortunately, there are various resources for meeting this need. There are Catholic charismatic prayer meetings, ACTS groups, Cursillo groups, bible studies, the Catholic Daughters, the Legion of Mary, groups specifically for men, groups specifically for women, groups specifically for youth, the Knights of Columbus, and several other groups that provide a source of fellowship for Catholics. These are all good if the business part of the meeting doesn't overshadow the fellowship.

Catholics need to take advantage of these opportunities and grow in a relationship of spiritual friendship and trust. It's also within the context of a community that we can discover and grow in the gifts God has given us. As we grow in fellowship, our familiarity will make it easier to sense where there is a need, and how the Holy Spirit may be calling us to meet that need.

God wants us to have fellowship with each other, because he wants us to share in the love of the Father, the Son, and the Holy Spirit. The Trinity is a fellowship of love that is so perfect they are one. This is what God is calling us to.⁹⁶

Through the power of the Holy Spirit, God is calling us to live in a fellowship of love with each other. Sin keeps us from this, but as we grow in fellowship with each other and with Jesus we will begin to experience the kind of fellowship God wants us to have.

Jesus's Praying Hands

On the other side of the cross is Jesus's left hand. Many times, before Jesus was crucified, his left hand would be joined with his right when he went to his Father in prayer. Prayer was important for Jesus, and we can see in scripture where he went off by himself to be alone with the Father.⁹⁷ If Jesus himself felt the need for prayer, surely, we need it even more.

Prayer is essential to the spiritual life because it keeps us in touch with God, who is our power source. It reminds us that God is always present and, if we take the time to listen, will enable us to hear his voice more clearly.

---

96 "That they may all be one, as you, Father, are in me and I in you, that they also may be in us, that the world may believe that you sent me" (John 17:20).
97 For instance: Mark 1:35, Matthew 14:23, Luke 6:12, Luke 22:41–44, John 12:27–28, John 11:41–42.

At rock bottom, prayer is simply talking with God. Note that prayer is not just talking to God, it's talking with God. Too often prayer is seen as something we do rather than something we participate in. When we share something of ourselves with God, we need to listen to him respond. This is how we grow in our relationship with God. We share ourselves with him, and he shares himself with us. This is basically what prayer is all about.

Although there are many different types of prayer, the most basic form is called spontaneous prayer. This is prayer that springs from the depths of the heart. Whether someone is immediately in need of God's presence or offering their day to him, spontaneous prayer expresses our specific intentions to him. It encourages the one praying to reflect on what they want to say and put their thoughts into words.

Prayers that have been prewritten or memorized are very good too, provided the words are prayed and not just recited. It's very easy just to recite the words of a prayer we're familiar with without paying attention to what we're saying. The words are said but the mind is somewhere else. When this happens, the worst thing we can do is get angry and start condemning ourselves for it.

One way of responding to the distractions is to remind ourselves of the one to whom we're praying and move on.[98]

---

98 This is the suggestion given by St. Teresa of Avila on praying the Our Father in chapter 24, #5 of *The Way of Perfection*. This can also be applied to any vocal prayer.

Vocal prayers recited in this way can lead to deeper levels of prayer, so there's nothing wrong with them at all.

But spontaneous prayer is like having a conversation with a friend. It's sharing ourselves with God and listening to God share himself with us. For those who might not have a whole lot to say, though, it's going to make for a very short prayer: "Hi, God, this is Deacon Mike. We'll see you tomorrow." That might be a bit of an exaggeration, but there is a guide for praying spontaneously. It's a prayer outline called ACTS.

The letter A is for

Adoration

After taking a moment to still our minds and be aware that God is truly present with us, we begin with adoration. This is simply praising God: "God, I praise you, I love you, I worship you, I adore you! You are everything to me! Help me to surrender my life more fully to you! God, you are the king of kings and the lord of lords. The entire universe is in your hands! I praise you for my family and all the wonderful things you've given me!"

Remember that praise is one of the purposes for the gift of tongues. This is a good place for its use if one desires. It's praising God for the wonder of creation, the wonder of his love, and the wonder of his awesome power!

In Psalm 22:3 we're told: "Yet thou art holy, enthroned on the praises of Israel" (RSV). Another way of saying this is that God is present in the praises of his people. As we adore and worship God with our praises, we can begin to sense his presence within us. Adoration is an awesome way to begin prayer.

The C is for

Contrition

We call to mind our sins and ask Jesus for forgiveness. Instead of just listing our sins we need to talk them over with Jesus. Ask him to help you understand why some sins are committed repeatedly. Can you make a plan for avoiding these sins, such as staying away from people and situations that draw you into their grasp? Are there things you can do to strengthen your determination not to sin? And if you're asking for Jesus's forgiveness, have you forgiven others or asked them to forgive you?

In addition to the sins we have committed through our actions, we can also be guilty of sin by *not* doing something. These are called "sins of omission." Not saying our daily prayers, not helping someone in need, or avoiding an opportunity to serve are examples of sins of omission. We need to remember these sins when confessing them to Jesus. Of course, this does not replace the sacrament of reconciliation. Its purpose here is to reflect on our sins before going to confession.

In summary, then, these are some points of conversation between you and Jesus that can come up with the prayer of contrition.[99]

The T is for

Thanksgiving

In this prayer we thank God for all the gifts he's given us. We can thank him for the day, the sunset, our health, our families, creation, our job, our faith, and on and on. We can also be thankful for some of the things we gave him adoration for as well. But it's also important that we don't leave out those situations and circumstances that we're not completely overjoyed about. In 1 Thessalonians 5:18 we're told: "In all circumstances give thanks, for this is the will of God for you in Christ Jesus" (NAB).

This doesn't mean God wills bad things to happen to us. God's will for us, rather, is to praise him *in all* circumstances. When bad things happen to us, we can still praise God! We praise him because he is God.

We praise him because we know he still loves us and is in control of our lives. We praise him because we know that in spite of the situation, "With God all things are possible!"

---

99 This is similar to the General Examination of Conscience outlined by St. Ignatius of Loyola #24–43 of the Spiritual Exercises.

(Matthew 19:26). And finally, we praise God because, "We know that all things work for good for those who love God" (Romans 8:28, NAB).

We might not *feel* this level of thanksgiving, but we thank God anyway to keep our faith from crumbling. We thank God because it is by trusting in him that our faith will be strengthened! We thank God because, whether we can understand it or not, it is what God has commanded us to do.

The S is for

Supplication

This can also be called a prayer of petition. It is in this part of the prayer that we make our requests to God. This can be a prayer for ourselves, for someone else, or for a situation we're concerned about. God, of course, is aware of our needs and what we're going to pray even before we ask him. But God wants us to ask so we'll praise him when he grants our requests.

In Luke 18:1–8 Jesus tells a story about a widow who came to an unjust judge to give her a decision against her adversary. Initially, the unjust judge wasn't going to do anything about it. He had no concern for the feelings of others or of the wrath of God. But because of the lady's persistence he finally gave in to her request.

Jesus's point was that God will surely hear and answer all our prayers. But there are many who will claim that God has never answered their prayers. How can this be the case? Either God does answer prayer, or he doesn't.

The problem is that when we pray, we are looking at one microscopic part of our lives, whereas God sees the whole thing. He's looking at the whole of who we are: past, present, and to come. God doesn't will for evil, bad, or inconvenient things to happen to us. This is the fault of sin and free will. But God can work for good even in trials.

And sometimes, God is calling us to participate with him in answering our prayer. In chapter 8, I asked God to provide for our financial need like he had for the lady we interviewed on the radio. God's response to me was to finish college so I could get a better job. Sometimes God will give us what we ask for by having us do something about it.

There are also those times when we cannot understand why God doesn't answer prayer in a specific way. It's in these times we're called to put our trust in him and give our faith a chance to grow. It's the same when we pray for others, local, national, and/or world situations. We never know the effect our prayers are going to have on what we're praying for, but we know that God is faithful in answering our prayers.[100] The important thing is to pray and to never give up hope.

---

[100] "Therefore, I tell you, all that you ask for in prayer, believe that you will receive it and it shall be yours" (Mark 11:24).

These four ways of being crucified with Christ can help us grow in the Spirit-filled life. If we're not used to practicing these spiritual disciplines, getting started and maintaining them is going to be a sacrifice. But once the habit develops, it will be hard to go a day without them. And the neat thing about this is the more we're crucified with Christ, the more of Christ's joy we're going to experience.[101]

---

[101] "For as we share abundantly in Christ's sufferings, so through Christ we share abundantly in comfort too" (2 Corinthians 1:5).

Questions for Thought and Discussion

1. "I have been crucified with Christ; yet I live, no longer I, but Christ lives in me" (Galatians 2:19b–20, NAB). What does this text mean to you personally? How can you apply it to everyday life?

2. How can we crucify our thought life? How can we renew our thought life?

3. How would your life change if your feet were crucified with Jesus's feet on the cross? Or how has your life been changed since your feet were crucified with Jesus's feet on the cross?

4. Have you ever sensed the Holy Spirit calling you to serve in a particular way? Did you respond? What happened?

5. What kind of fellowship are you engaged in right now?

6. What does it mean to share in Trinitarian love?

7. Why is adoration a good place to begin prayer?

8. Give some examples not covered in the book of sins of omission. Why is it important to confess these sins as well as those we actually commit?

9. What are some ways we can cooperate with the Holy Spirit to bring about our own crucifixion?

CHAPTER 15
Spiritual Warfare

The Dream

My wife once had a dream that is a good example of what we go through in spiritual warfare. She said, "I was hiding behind Jesus, occasionally peeping out to see these demons that were laughing at me. They were making horrible, shrieking noises and they kept telling me, "So, you call yourself a Christian. Okay, Christian, come out from behind your Jesus. Let's see how strong you are."

They continued laughing at me. I was trembling with fear, my knees were shaking, and my heart was beating fast. But they dared not even get close because they were afraid of Jesus. They wanted me to come out from behind Jesus so my eyes would be taken off him. So, I said, "Without God I can do nothing."

As soon as I said that, I saw light and fire in the shape of a sword coming out of Jesus's eyes. The demons screamed with fright and disappeared. Jesus remained comforting me."

The Devil is a Liar

Every day Christians are involved in spiritual warfare, whether they're aware of it or not. We know there's a devil out there because he's mentioned in sacred scripture, and it's his job to tempt us to sin. But most people don't worry a whole lot about him, nor does he worry a great deal about them.

He doesn't have to. He's influenced our culture, and our culture just follows his lead. Some may not even believe the devil exists. This doesn't bother the devil at all. The less people believe in him, the easier it is for them to be tempted by him. But there are several places in the gospels where Jesus encountered the devil.[102]

The first instance is when Jesus was tempted by the devil in the wilderness.[103] After this, Jesus delivered several people from various symptoms of demonic possession (Luke 4:41.) In John 10:18, Jesus said that he saw "Satan fall like lightning from the sky." Jesus was adamant about the existence of the devil.

The devil's reality is even mentioned in the Catechism of the Catholic Church.[104] They are created beings (CCC 391) who have rebelled against God (CCC 392) and strive

---

102 See Matthew 4:1–10, Matthew 8:28–34, Mark 3:11, Mark 9:25–26, Luke 4:33–35, Luke 10:18, John 8:44.
103 Matthew 4:1–11 and Luke 4:1–12.
104 See CCC 391, 392, 1237, 1707, 1708, 2851. For more examples see "Demon" in the index of the Catechism.

to destroy God's plan for creation (CCC 395). He does this by convincing us to turn away from God.

In John 8:44, Jesus tells us the devil "is a liar and the father of lies" (NAB). We can see this from the very beginning when he lied to Eve about eating the forbidden fruit. The devil (characterized as a snake) convinced Eve that God had lied to them, and they would be happiest if they disobeyed his command. It wasn't long after they gave in to the devil's temptation, that they discovered it was the devil who had lied to them.

The same is true with us. God has told us if we follow him and keep his commands, we will have an abundant life (John 10:10.) [105] But the devil tells us differently. Through the media and culture in general, the devil has convinced many people that God is not powerful enough to make them happy or give them the fulfillment they're seeking. The alternative the devil gives them is any lifestyle that contradicts a relationship with God.

The problem with this is if someone rejects God, they're never going to be at peace. They're constantly seeking for more pleasure, more material goods, and more applause to fill their emptiness. Their emptiness will never be filled outside of God because we have been created for God (CCC 27.)

---

[105] "I came so that they might have life and have it more abundantly."

On the other hand, a relationship with God seeks to glorify and serve him alone. We may occasionally struggle with the devil's lies, but God will constantly draw us back to himself. I noticed this struggle in myself as our state and Church started allowing groups to meet following the pandemic.

One of the first things we did was resume our prayer meeting. We felt people were hungering for spiritual growth and were especially in need of Christian fellowship. We got the word out and began preparing for our prayer meeting just as we always had done. We prepared the music, PowerPoint, teaching, and set up the chairs.

For several months very few people attended our prayer group. COVID was still around, and people were hesitant about meeting as a group. One day I began wondering why I was putting forth all that effort. Maybe it wasn't God's will for us to meet. Perhaps I should just end the prayer group altogether. It didn't seem like God was answering my prayers, and I was going through all that work for nothing. I began to feel angry and out of peace.

Suddenly another thought came to me: Who was I preparing the prayer meeting for anyway? I was preparing it for Jesus. And if all Jesus wanted of me was to prepare the prayer meeting then that's what I was going to do. Through God's way of looking at things, my anger was turned into peace and joy.

This may be a small example, but it shows how Satan works. He gets us to focus on a lie, convinces us the lie is truth, and before we know it, we've bought into the lie.

The devil wants us to focus on the situation and on ourselves. But if we keep our eyes on Jesus, as Kathy learned in her dream, Jesus will take care of the demons for us. One of the best weapons God has given us for this is scripture. (I have provided a list of twenty promises for spiritual warfare at the end of the chapter.) The text from John 10:10 [106] and 1 Corinthians 2:9 [107] are good for reminding us of God's promise to make us fully happy.

Another lie of the devil is that God doesn't love us. The truth is that God loves us so much he is constantly thinking about us and constantly drawing us closer to himself. Psalm 139:13–14 is a reminder of how intimately God knows us:

> You formed my inmost being;
> you knit me in my mother's
> womb.
> I praise you because I am
> wonderfully made;
> wonderful are your works!
> My very self you know (NAB).

---

[106] "A thief come only to steal and slaughter and destroy; I came so that they might have life and have it more abundantly" (NAB).
[107] "What no eye has seen, nor ear heard, nor the heart of man conceived, what God has prepared for those who love him" (RSV).

In Isaiah 49:16, God tells us, "See, upon the palms of my hands I have engraved you" (NAB).

The devil will tell us we're never going to change so we may as well just give in to a life of sin. But Philippians 4:13 tells us that we can do all things through Christ who strengthens us! The devil is also very condemning. Worrying over a past or more recent sin will give the devil an open door to start condemning us. He'll try to convince us that our sin is unforgivable.

When these thoughts come to us, we can respond with Romans 8:1: "Hence, now there is no condemnation for those who are in Christ Jesus" (NAB). When we sin, we need to repent and move on, but condemning ourselves is what the devil wants.

Sometimes the devil will catch us in an argument with someone, and he'll give us thoughts that will make us even angrier. We may begin to see the other person as the epitome of evil, increasing our anger towards them. The devil convinces us that they're entirely wrong, and there's no way we can ever be reconciled with them. In fact, the devil will convince us that our joy is going to come from being angry.

But Ephesians 6:12, tells us, "For our struggle is not with flesh and blood but with the principalities, with the powers, with the world rulers of this present darkness, with the evil spirits in the heavens" (NAB). The devil will try to convince us that the enemy is other people when, in fact, he is the true enemy. He is the one trying to destroy us.

> Our struggle is not with flesh and blood but...with the evil spirits in the heavens.

At this point, we can continue listening to the devil's lies, or we can stop and let God take over. If we let God take over, then we are making a choice to love. In Matthew 5:44, Jesus tells us to love our enemies, and in John 13:34–35, Jesus said, "I give you a new commandment: love one another. As I have loved you, so you also should love one another" (NAB). The devil's greatest enemy is love.

Who Do We Want to Follow?

Every day in a variety of circumstances, spiritual warfare is asking us who we want to follow. In Matthew 6:24, we're told: "No one can serve two masters. He will either hate one and love the other or be devoted to one and despise the other" (NAB). Spiritual warfare is about deciding whose side we want to be on.

It seems like this would be an obvious choice, "For the wages of sin is death, but the gift of God is eternal life in Christ Jesus our Lord" (Romans 6:23, NAB). But the reason it's so easy for us to believe the devil's lies is because he makes them sound so attractive to us. Our fallen, carnal nature is drawn to the very things the devil presents to us: sensual pleasure, materialism, self-indulgence, etc. But because we have free will, we can choose not to give in to these temptations.

Whenever a trial comes in our lives, the devil is right there, ready to pounce on us. He tries to convince us that if God really loved us, or if he existed at all, he would not have let this terrible circumstance happen to us. Our natural tendency is to focus on the situation. This will cause us to feel discouraged and depressed. The devil will try to make the situation seem even worse, thereby increasing our bad feelings.

Initially, we're going to want to go with the bad feelings. But as soon as we're aware of them, we need to listen to what God has promised us. In Romans 8:28, we're promised that "all things work for good for those who love God" (NAB). And in James 1:2, we are told that trials should be an occasion for pure joy because they help us grow in faith. It's all a matter of looking at the situation through God's eyes.

We need to constantly be leery of the devil's attacks because he "is prowling around like a roaring lion looking for [someone] to devour" (1 Peter 5:8, NAB). As soon as we let down our guard or open ourselves up, he is there for the attack. But once we recognize his attack, we need to be ready with a defense.

In James 4:7, we're told, "Resist the devil and he will flee" (NAB). The more we resist his attacks, the more power we will have over him. That's why it's good to have a plan ahead of time rather than coming up with something after we're already under attack. That's where familiarity with God's promises comes in.

Weapons of Defense

The best way to maintain a scriptural arsenal of God's promises is to put them to memory. This way, the Holy Spirit can bring a text to our minds as soon as one is needed. The second-best way is to read and reflect on the text over and over again. This will keep the text in the subconscious, allowing the Holy Spirit to remind us of it when it's needed.

Whether the scriptures are being memorized or not, a different promise can be written on index cards and referred to throughout the day. This will help for both memorization and familiarity.

As I mentioned before, there are twenty texts that can be used for this at the end of the chapter. There are many more texts that can be used, but these are given as a sample. In whichever way we familiarize ourselves with God's promises, it is important to make them a part of our spiritual arsenal.

The devil is not more powerful than God, and we have been given weapons to fight against him. Indeed, one of the scriptural promises is that "we are more than conquerors through him who loved us" (Romans 8:37, RSV). We already have victory through Jesus Christ. We just have to stand in our victory.

Be Clothed in the Armor of God

A good way of standing in victory is to clothe ourselves every day with the armor of God. The text this comes from is Ephesians 6:13-17:

> Therefore, put on the armor of God, that you may be able to resist on the evil day, having done everything, to hold your ground. So stand fast with your loins girded in truth, clothed with righteousness as a breastplate, and your feet shod in readiness for the gospel of peace. In all circumstances, hold faith as a shield, to quench all the flaming arrows of the evil one (NAB).

As soon as we begin the day, we need to realize that we're in a spiritual war zone. We're going to be attacked, and we need to be ready for it. Jesus is the center of our lives, and our focus needs to be on him, not on the devil.

Still, we need to be ready through whatever means are available to us: Prayer, daily Mass, spiritual reading, sacramentals, praying in tongues, etc. This will help us stand our ground against the devil's attacks because it will keep our focus on God. And then we need to put on the armor of protection that God has given us.

In verse 14, we're told to keep our loins girded in truth.

> **Keep your loins girded in truth.**

St. Paul is referring to the belt that a soldier would clothe himself with. It was the center of his armor. It kept the upper and lower parts together, and it was from the belt that his sword hung. To have his belt girded was to be ready for the fight.

Knowing the promises of God and the teachings of our faith are the truths we need to cling to when defending ourselves. Having this knowledge makes us ready for the fight. Remember that in most cases, it will not be our job to attack the devil but to defend ourselves against his attacks.

Verse 14 also talks about "being clothed with righteousness as a breastplate." The breastplate of armor covered the heart and the internal organs of the soldier. It gave protection to these important areas of the body. The breastplate of righteousness is faith in Jesus Christ. We may not always be righteous, but Jesus Christ is.

One of the devil's greatest weapons is to attack us because of our sin, our shortcomings, and our weaknesses. This causes us to feel discouraged and depressed. When the devil attacks us in this way, we need to remind ourselves that we are weak, but it's Jesus Christ who has saved us. He is the breastplate of righteousness. If we keep ourselves clothed with this knowledge, we will be victorious over the devil.

Verse 15 tells us to keep our "feet shod in readiness for the gospel of peace" (NAB). The sandals of a Roman soldier laced up the sides of his legs gave him security in battle. Our spiritual shoes need to make us feel firm in our stand against the evil one.

Often when adversity comes our way, we become defeated with a variety of emotions: discouragement, depression, disappointment, anxiety, nervousness, and so on. We're not able to stand firm because we're shaking in our boots.

> Keep your feet shod in readiness with the gospel of peace.

In John 14:27, Jesus said, "Peace I leave with you; my peace I give to you" (NAB). We must claim that peace and focus on it as much as we can. If we know the truth and have clothed ourselves in Jesus Christ, we should be able to stand on a foundation of peace.

The devil's lie, though, will be that there's no reason to be at peace. He'll have us focus on the situation, blow it out of proportion, and convince us there's no hope at all. It's then that we need to believe God's promise to us in scripture: "Resist the devil and he will flee from you" (NAB). We need to focus on God's promises and take our focus off the situation.

As we continue to make a choice to focus on Jesus (because we might not feel like it), we will begin to gain strength over the devil's temptations. We might even want to start praising God and thanking him *for* the situation. We thank him, confident that we are going to see his glory through it.

> Hold faith as a shield

But if one is still not able to find peace, they might want to seek additional help. There may, for instance, be a need for the sacrament of reconciliation. There may be a need for professional psychological help.

The purpose of this chapter is just to make people aware of the reality of spiritual warfare and some of the basics for dealing with it. Anything beyond that is outside the scope of this chapter.

Verse 16 says, "In all circumstances, hold faith as a shield, to catch all the flaming arrows of the evil one" (NAB). This shield was held by the soldier to give added protection against the arrows of the enemy. This is what our faith in Jesus does. When we're being attacked, the first question we need to ask ourselves is, "Who do I have my faith in? Do I have my faith in my own ability, or is my faith in God?"

Proverbs 3:5–6 tells us to trust in the Lord with all our heart, and not to rely on our own understanding. We are often going to fail, and others are going to fail us as well. But God will never fail us. In Psalm 23:1, the psalmist says, "The Lord is my shepherd; there is nothing I lack" (NAB). If our faith and our trust are in God, what more do we need?

Verse 17 says, "And take the helmet of salvation." The helmet protects the warrior's

> Take the helmet of salvation.

brain, the center of his thinking. The devil's army is constantly trying to shape our thinking or change the way we look at things. His goal is to convince us that everything we have been taught about goodness and holiness is wrong and should be shunned. What is right are those things that we had previously been taught to be wrong. It's like the people Isaiah was speaking to when he said:

> Ah! Those who call evil good
> and good evil,
> who change darkness to
> light, and light into
> darkness,
> who change bitter to sweet
> and sweet to bitter!
> (Isaiah 5:20, NAB)

Through media, social pressure, advertisement, entertainment and so on, we are told that Christian values were for a former time. Since they are not in sync with contemporary, progressive thinking, they need to be avoided and discouraged. We need to fill our minds with the word of God.

Verse 17 also tells us the word of God is the sword of the Spirit. This is what we use to fight against the attacks on our faith and values. We use this knowledge to give an answer to others, but even more to fight against the devil's attack on our minds.

> The sword of the Spirit is the word of God.

Some people like to check their spiritual armor in the morning when they pray. They read the text and reflect on the presence of each armor part in their arsenal for the day. Is everything in its place? Are my loins girded in truth? Am I clothed with the breastplate of righteousness? Am I holding faith as a shield against the flaming arrows of the evil one? Have I put on the helmet of salvation by becoming familiar with the word of God? Am I learning how to use God's word to fight against spiritual attacks?

Every day we need to be ready for the devil's attacks because we are in a spiritual war zone. The only way we're going to survive is by learning how to use the weapons God has given us.

Questions for Thought and Discussion

1. Before this teaching, were you aware that you're living in a spiritual war zone?

2. Can you think of a time that you've been spiritually attacked? If it's not too personal, can you share this with the group?

3. In what ways can you see the devil trying to influence the cultural thinking of today?

4. How can the devil influence someone's thinking in an argument? Can you give a scripture to counter the devil's argument?

5. Can you give an example of the devil lying to our culture? What are the consequences of this lie?

6. What are some things we can do to gird our loins in truth?

7. How can we keep our feet shod for the gospel of peace?

8. Give some examples of the flaming arrows of the evil one. How does faith function as a shield against these?

9. Do you think most people in our culture believe in the devil? What do they think he's like? Do they think we should be concerned about him? Why do you think they believe this way?

CHAPTER 16
Scriptural Helps

For Spiritual Warfare

1. "Take delight in the Lord and he will give you the desires of your heart" (Psalm 37:4, RSV).

2. "I can do all things through him who strengthens me" (Philippians 4:13, RSV).

3. "I have said this to you, that in me you may have peace. In the world you will have tribulation; but be of good cheer. I have overcome the world" (John 16:33, RSV).

4. "But whoever drinks the water I shall give will never thirst; the water I shall give will become in him a spring of water welling up to eternal life" (John 4:14, NAB).

5. "Weeping may tarry for the night, but joy comes with the morning" (Psalm 30:5, RSV).

6. "And behold, I am with you always, until the end of the age" (Matthew 28:20, NAB).

7. "He will wipe every tear from their eye, and there will be no more death or mourning, wailing or pain, for the old order has passed away" (Revelation 21:4, NAB).

8. Are not two sparrows sold for a small coin? Yet not one of them falls to the ground without your Father's knowledge. Even all the hairs on your head are counted. So, do not be afraid; you are worth more than many sparrows" (Matthew 10:29–31, NAB).

9. "So do not worry and say, 'What are we to eat? or 'What are we to wear?' All these things the pagans seek. Your heavenly Father knows that you need them all. But seek first the kingdom of God and his righteousness, and all these things will be given you besides" (Matthew 7:31–33, NAB).

10. "A thief comes only to steal and slaughter and destroy; I came so that they [you] might have life and have it more abundantly" (John 10:10, NAB).

11. "Behold, I stand at the door and knock. If anyone hears my voice and opens the door, I will enter his house and dine with him, and he with me" (Revelation 4:20, NAB).

12. "Can a mother forget her infant, be without tenderness for the child of her womb? Even should she forget, I will never forget you. See, upon the palms of my hands I have engraved you" (Isaiah 49:15–16, NAB).

13. "And whatever you ask in my name, I will do, so that the Father may be glorified in the Son. If you ask anything of me in my name, I will do it" (John 14:12–14, NAB).

14. "We know that in everything God works for good with those who love him" (Romans 8:28, RSV).

15. "Who shall separate us from the love of Christ? Shall tribulation, or distress, or persecution, or famine, or nakedness, or peril, or sword? . . . No, in all these things we are more than conquerors through him who loved us. For I am sure that neither death, nor life, nor angels, nor principalities, nor things present, nor things to come, nor powers, nor height, nor death, nor anything else in all creation, will be able to separate us from the love of God in Christ Jesus our Lord" (Romans 8:35 & 37–39, RSV).

16. "Why are you downcast, my soul; why do you groan within me? Wait for God, for I shall again praise him, my savior, and my God" (Psalm 42:6 NSB).

17. "Behold, I have given you the power to tread upon serpents and scorpions and upon the full force of the enemy and nothing shall harm you." (Luke 6:19 NAB)

18. "For our struggle is not with flesh and blood but with the principalities, with the powers, with the world rulers of the present darkness, with the evil spirits in the heavens." (Ephesians 6:12 NAB)

19. "Because you are precious in my eyes, because you are honored and I love you, I give men in exchange for you, peoples in return for your life. Do not be afraid, for I am with you." (Isaiah 43:4-5 JB)

20. "Resist the devil and he will flee from you." (James 4:7 NAB)

CHAPTER 17

The Invitation

On May 30, 1998, Saint Pope John Paul II gave a speech to nearly a million people involved with ecclesial movements and new ministries. At one point in the speech, he said,

> Today, I would like to cry out to all of you gathered here in St Peter's Square and to all Christians: Open yourselves docilely to the gifts of the Spirit! Accept gratefully and obediently the charisms which the Spirit never ceases to bestow on us! Do not forget that every charism is given for the common good—that is, for the benefit of the whole Church.[108]

Our task as Catholic Christians is to use the gifts God has given us to continue Jesus's ministry on earth. The whole world is hungering to meet Jesus, and our job is to bring Jesus to them. One of the ways God has prepared for us to do this is through the gifts of the Holy Spirit.

---

[108] Pope John Paull II, "For the World Congress of Ecclesial Movements and New Communities," (May 30, 1998), Vatican website.

Prayer to the Holy Spirit

O, Holy Spirit, grant that I may be sensitive to your guidance. Grant me the wisdom to see those things you want me to do and the courage to do them. Show me the gifts I have been given, enabling me to serve you through serving others. Use me as a source of bringing your miracles, your love, your healing, your peace, your hope, your joy, and your new life to others. Pour forth a fountain of living water within me so that I can share your living water with others. In Jesus's name. Amen

Bibliography

Augustine, St. *The City of God.* Translated by Gerald G. Walsh, S.J., Demetrius B. Zema, S.J., Grace Monahah, O.S.U., Daniel J. Honan. New York: Doubleday, 1958.

Bethge, Eberhard. *Dietric Bonhoeffer: A Biography.* Revised. Minneapolis. Fortress Press. 1999.

Bennett, Dennis J. *Nine O'Clock in the Morning.* Alachua: Bridge Logos, 1970.

*Catechism of the Catholic Church 2nd ed.*_United States Catholic Conference of Bishops. The Holy See: Librereia Editrice Vaticana, 2000.

Cieszinski, Joseph D. *Loaves and Fishes: Jesus and the Feeding of the Multitudes. Multiplication Stories of the Bible and the Church and Their Relevance Today.* Goleta: Queenship, 2016.

Collected Works of St. John of the Cross. Translated by Kieran Kavanaugh, OCD and Otilio Rodriguez, OCD. Washington, D.C.: Institute of Carmelite Studies, 1979.

Collected Works of St. Teresa of Avila, Vol. 2. Translated by Kieran Kavanaugh, OCD and Otilio Rodriguez, OCD. Washington, D.C.: Institute of Carmelite Studies, 1980.

Congar, Yves. *I Believe in the Holy Spirit.* Translated by David Smith. New York: Herder Crossroad, 2005.

Dulles, Avery, S.J. *Models of the Church.* New York: Doubleday, 1987.

Ensley, Eddie. *Sounds of Wonder: A Popular History of Speaking in Tongues in the Catholic Tradition.* New York/Ramsey: Paulist Press, 1977.

Flannery, Austin, ed., *Vatican Council II: The Conciliar and Postconciliar Documents.* Collegeville: Liturgical Press, 1996.

Fleming, David L. S.J., trans. and ed., *Spiritual Exercises of St. Ignatius of Loyola.* The Institute of Jesuit Sources, Saint Louis, MO. 1978.

Francis I. "Address to the Renewal in the Holy Spirit Movement," St. Peter's Square, Friday, July 3, 2015. The Holy See: Libreria Editrice Vaticana. Vatican website.

Gallagher-Mansfield, Patti. *As by A New Pentecost.* Steubenville: Franciscan University Press, 1992.

Ignatius of Loyola. *The Autobiography of St. Ignatius.* E-book. StreetLib Write

John XXIII. *Humanae Salutis,* #23. Dec. 25, 1961. The Holy See: Libreria Editrice Vaticana. Vatican website.

John Paul II. "Message of Pope John Paul II for the World Congress of Ecclesial Movements and New Communities," Saturday, 30 May 1998. The Holy See: Libreria Editrice Vaticana. Vatican website.

Kolodiejchuk, Brian, ed., *Mother Teresa: Come Be My Light: The Private Writings of the "Saint of Calcutta."* New York: Doubleday, 2007.

Life in the Spirit Seminars Team Manual Catholic Edition. Developed by the Word of God. Ann Arbor: Servant Books, 1979.

Linguistic Society of America. "How Many Languages Are There in the World?" https://www.linguisticsociety.org/content/how-many-languages-are-there-world

McDonnell, Kilian, and Montague, George T. *Christian Initiation and Baptism in the Holy Spirit: Evidence from the First Eight Centuries.* Collegeville: The Liturgical Press, 1994.

Metaxes, Eric. *Bonhoeffer: Pastor, Martyr, Prophet, Spy.* Thomas Nelson. 2010.

National Directory for Catechesis. United States Conference of Catholic Bishops, Washington, D.C., 2005.

Paul VI. "Salvifici Doloris: On the Christian Meaning of Human Suffering, 1984." The Holy See: Libreria Editrice Vaticana. Vatican website.

Bibliography

Pius X. *Vehementer Nos: On the French Law of Separation*, #8, Feb.11, 1906. The Holy See: Libreria Editrice Vaticana. Vatican website.

Proctor, Patricia. *201 Inspirational Stories of the Eucharist*. Spokane, Washington. Called by Joy. 2005.

Rite of Christian Initiation of Adults. National Conference of Catholic Bishops. New York: Catholic Book Publishing Co., 1988

Suenens, Joseph Léon. *A New Pentecost?* New York: Seabury Press, 1975.

Wilkerson, David. *The Cross and the Switchblade*. New Jersey. Spire Books. 1963.

CPSIA information can be obtained
at www.ICGtesting.com
Printed in the USA
BVHW040806091122
651118BV00006B/19